OHNE WORTE

This twelfth publication in the series
"Collected Writings of the Orpheus Institute"
is edited by William Brooks

OHNE WORTE

Vocality and Instrumentality in 19th-Century Music

Edoardo Torbianelli
Jeanne Roudet
Jean-Pierre Bartoli
Douglas Seaton
Hubert Moßburger

COLLECTED WRITINGS OF THE
ORPHEUS
INSTITUTE

Leuven University Press
2014

CONTENTS

PREFACE

In this volume I am an interloper. I have arrived late in the process, after much of the work had been done by the chapter authors and by Darla Crispin. Darla subsequently left the Orpheus Institute for a life in the north; I am grateful, as ever, for her advice, her intelligence, and her friendship. But the volume began even earlier, at the eighth Orpheus Academy, held 29 March to 1 April 2010, at which the papers here were first presented, admired, and critiqued. Along the way, material came and went, as the authors demonstrated both patience and resourcefulness. A contribution from Jean-Pierre Bartoli and Jeanne Roudet grew into an excellent book (Bartoli and Roudet 2013) and so is not represented in this collection; other papers mutated as research and publications continued. I am grateful for the tolerance and patience all the authors displayed as the book stuttered forward through a series of reviews and revisions. It should not have been that way, but it seems that it always is.

I was trained first as a pianist and then as a vocalist, growing up with Chopin and Mendelssohn on the music rack, Schumann and Brahms in my book bag. So I come to *Ohne Worte* rather as a wanderer returning home: the faces are familiar and much-loved, but I myself have changed so much that I hardly know how to address them. My route has taken me, among other paths, on a circumnavigation of the world often called "experimental music," with particular attention to American composers. By geography and culture as well as chronology these figures would seem to be considerably distant from the figures present in this volume. Yet I would claim a connection; further, I claim that connection forms the continuity between the Orpheus Academy, now nearly a half-decade past, and the current Orpheus focus on the nature of experiment in artistic research. In this short preface I will try to draw out a few of the threads that form that connection, that allow this collection to speak—powerfully!—to me, today.

The grandfather of American experimentalism is Charles Ives, whose work serves both as a summation of the nineteenth century and a precursor of things to come. A foundation stone of Ives's music, sometimes overlooked, was his thorough knowledge of nineteenth-century European lieder (Block and Burkholder 1996; Morgan 1997). The *114 Songs* (1922) contain four settings of German texts, made at Yale at Horatio Parker's behest. These are both pastiches and worthy departures, demonstrating at once Ives's complete absorption of European harmonic practice and a distinctively American approach to textual and formal continuity. But Ives's engagement with European vocality and instrumentality goes much deeper than copybook exercises. His *Essays before a Sonata*, written after his compositional initiatives had ended, open with one of the questions that underlie much of the present volume: "How far is anyone justified, be he an authority or a layman, in expressing or trying to express in terms of music (in sounds, if you like) the value of anything, material, moral, intellectual, or spiritual, which is usually expressed in terms other than music?" (Ives 1962, 3). And his major works—not just the "Concord" Sonata, but the Third and Fourth Symphonies, the violin sonatas, the orchestral sets—demonstrate that he himself was willing to attempt such expressions broadly and deeply.

It is less of a leap than one might think: I would argue that one of the summative presentations of the entire Romantic preoccupation with the relation of words and music, vocality and instrumentality, was made by Charles Ives. Ives's philosophical grandparent was Emerson; and his philosophical stepbrothers were pragmatists—William James and John Dewey. At the same time Ives has been positioned as the ultimate ancestor of what became called American experimentalism. It is thus possible to propose that experimental composers like John Cage are the oblique inheritors of music "ohne worte"—that the dialectic between freedom and discipline in Cage's music and writings has its source in the Romantic dialectic between feeling and expression.[1]

1. To demonstrate the historical basis for this assertion is well beyond the scope of this preface. In addition to a proper genealogy of musical pragmatism, it requires, a deconstruction of the "other" Cage, the Buddhist, "Eastern" Cage. For a start on the former, see Brooks (2007 and 2009); for the latter, see Crooks (2011).

Dewey (1859–1952) was a near-contemporary of Ives (1874–1954), and, like Ives, his culminating work *Art as Experience* (1934) came rather late in his career. There he argues that experience is not a matter of mere sensation but a set of relations that obtain between the active self, discovering and exploring the world, and the receptive self, perceiving and understanding it: what Dewey calls the relations of "doing and undergoing" (44). And art is part of experience; it "unites the very same relation of doing and undergoing, outgoing and incoming energy. . . . [B]ecause of selection of just the aspects and traits that contribute to their interpenetration of each other, the product is a work of aesthetic art" (48). To return for a moment to the discourse on "experiment" at the Orpheus Institute, Dewey is arguing for a kind of "exploratory experimentation," a meandering model for artistic endeavour that reaches back to Goethe and was one of the streams that flowed through the Romantic landscape.[2]

OHNE WORTE

And with this we are led directly into the contents of *Ohne Worte*.

In "Playing with Images: Character and Emotion in the Age of Romanticism," Edoardo Torbianelli plunges into the inner world of feelings and imagination, arguing that technical skill in execution, no matter how historically informed, is insufficient to render the essence of Romantic piano music. For him, the "voice" and the guiding images are personal and interior; they interact with the score and instrument (both public and exterior) to produce a meaningful, emotionally charged performance. The performer's body, in this case, is the transducer, the medium for the interpenetration of outer world and inner self: it embodies and conveys the performer's understanding and at the same time responds to the demands of the environment.

In "'Inner Voices' and 'Deep Combinations': Robert Schumann's Approach to Romantic Polyphony," Hubert Moßburger takes us

2. "Exploratory experimentation" has been explored in the writings of Friedrich Steinle, who has also traced its roots in Goethe's thought; see Steinle (1997) and Ribe and Steinle (2002).

from Torbianelli's inner, performative states to the representation of the "hidden" self by means of "inner voices" and polyphonic interconnections. He analyses the expression of a particular kind of aesthetic impulse in Schumann's music—the desire to create "deep combinations" that underpin and transcend surface features. Like Torbianelli (and like Dewey), he postulates an "outer" world, public and accessible—the sung melody, the explicit text—and juxtaposes this with an interior, shadowy domain of unheard melody and inferred content. This is a pre-performance world, and in that sense Moßburger stresses primarily the "undergoing" half of Dewey's dialectic; but as he demonstrates, the score that results not only manifests that world but imposes its own demands for performers, opening a window for a music that is not only beyond words but—to some extent—beyond sound itself.

On the other hand, Jeanne Roudet's chapter, "Frédéric Chopin, Clara Schumann, and the Singing Piano School," is solidly grounded in Dewey's "doing." She reveals how singers sang, how pianists played, the nature of the instruments and their effects—all eminently practical matters, with clear mappings between vocality and instrumental performance that are drawn from a wide variety of sources. Yet there remains an underlying concern with "undergoing." The difference between Liszt's playing and that of Chopin and Clara Schumann is not just a matter of technique; it reveals a fundamental distinction between outer-directed acts, undertaken because they are known to be effective, and acts arising from the inner self, from the "voice" of the performer. The "singing piano school" is more than a way of playing; it accomplishes in performance the kind of "deep combinations" that Moßburger traced in composition, by bringing inner and outer, doing and undergoing, into an interactive equilibrium.

The second half of this collection of essays moves beyond the piano and its literature to consider broader realms: instrumental music in general and its relation to voices that not only sing but also tell a tale. If the first three chapters offer us valuable guides to our own "doing," the last three help us towards a more satisfying "undergoing."

Jean-Pierre Bartoli scrutinises "Vocal Patterns in the Themes of Berlioz's Instrumental Music." He embraces fully what Wieck (as summarised by Roudet) might have characterised as merely rhetorical, demonstrating that in the hands of an imaginative composer like Berlioz rhetorical devices—translated to musical terms—provide a surer guide to the creation of innovative musical utterances (themes) than the mere disposition of formal elements. Our feelings are intrinsically unbalanced, and the rhetoric needed to capture such feelings is unbalanced as well; hence the irregular construction of Berlioz's melodies, and hence their unorthodox power. Hence also the lineage that Bartoli traces in vocal music of all sorts, from Beethoven's *Fidelio* to commonplace French romances: the voice is, quite literally, an "inner" instrument, and it is a natural conduit for the moment-to-moment irregularities of experience. Dewey followed William James in asserting that consciousness was not apart from the world but a part of it; our experiences form parts of a stream of consciousness that folds back upon itself unpredictably but inevitably. An "experience" is constituted when—like a Berlioz theme—we find a narrative, an extended moment that is complete and satisfying in itself.

Douglass Seaton extends that argument beyond the construction of themes in considering "Plot and Narrative in Mendelssohn's Chamber Music for Strings and Piano." His distinction between plot and narrative is crucial: plot is external, explicit, made up of things and places and times. From a Deweyan perspective, plot is something we *do*. Narrative, on the other hand, is internal, hidden, and personal—a property deriving from a composer's "voice" (in Torbianelli's usage). We cannot point to the narrator's voice, manipulate or confine it; we sense it by other means, and we integrate it into our understanding. Narrative would seem to be something we *undergo*. Seaton's double framework enables an analysis of Mendelssohn's chamber music that is neither reductive nor metaphorical; rather, it moves freely and irregularly between an outer world of themes and keys and an inner one of personas and subjectivities. It treats the musical work as both a product and an instance of *experience*, in Dewey's sense; and the analysis is itself an exposition of a different experience, that of the listener. Both involve—both require—an interpenetration of self and other, an inflow and outgo in which sensorial information precipitates an understanding that itself becomes part of the sensed world.

Finally, Hubert Moßburger returns to examine "Robert Schumann's Poetic Paraphrases: Analytical Implications." His detailed treatment of Schumann's writings, textual and musical, allows us to trace Schumann's "voice" as articulated in "poetics" and the importance of these concepts both to a composer's working method and to a listener's auditory comprehension. Poetic paraphrases move beyond metaphoric exegesis to become artistic expressions in a parallel domain. Moßburger distinguishes three types of musical analysis, and once again these would seem to be situated on the spectrum between doing and undergoing. A technical analysis is very much external, concerned with objects and their properties; a poetic paraphrase is largely internal, arising from the summative personal experience of the perceiver. These are mediated by a third type of analysis, the "musico-linguistic," which moves freely between the poles, mapping sonic properties into internal states. A full understanding of a work requires the use of the full spectrum of possibilities, the technical leading to concrete acts, the poetic engendering imaginative re-creations. Moßburger's surprising conclusion brings the entire volume entirely back to the present day and to experimental music, justifying in retrospect the exploratory experimentation undertaken by all five authors.

This brief summary of the six chapters in *Ohne Worte* is neither dispassionate nor universal. Rather it is itself a demonstration of vocality, subjectivity, voice: I discover John Dewey and Charles Ives in what I have read not because *they* are there but because *I* am. Each of you, reading this volume, will likewise bring your "inner voice" to bear; we all of us sing along, each in our own way, creating an unstructured harmony that results to some extent from the shared reality with which we interpenetrate. And with this image, this singing inner voice, this poetic paraphrase, I am reminded again of Charles Ives. Perhaps I should give him the final word. Writing a "Postface" to his *114 Songs*, he gave "vocality"—song, if you will—an independent existence, freeing it not only from the limitations of voice and instrument but even from composerly control. We can but watch in admiration: "A song has a *few* rights, the same as other ordinary citizens. If it feels like walking along the left-hand side of the street, passing the door of physiology or sitting on the curb, why not let it? If it feels like kicking over an ash can, a poet's castle, or the prosodic law, will you stop it? . . . If it happens to feel like trying to fly where humans cannot fly, to sing what cannot be sung, to walk in a cave on all fours, or to tighten up its girth in blind hope and faith and try to scale mountains that are not, who shall stop it?—In short, must a song always be a song?" (Ives 1962, 130–31).

ENVOI

The interested reader will find generous reference lists at the end of each chapter. Many cite nineteenth-century sources (such as the *Neue Zeitschrift für Musik*) that have been accessed online, primarily in the remarkable repository at archive.org. We have not provided resource locators for these, largely for reasons of space; in general, a quick search of repositories will find the material more quickly than laborious copying of long browser codes. With foreign-language sources, Orpheus follows the editorial practice of using existing translations, when possible, rather than making new ones. Since subtleties of language are especially important in this case, however, we have included the original text in a footnote in most instances.

I am deeply indebted to many people who have contributed to this publication—to the authors, first and foremost, for their patience with the many delays and their willingness to revisit their essays time and again. Ed Crooks and Mark Hutchinson provided exceptional editorial assistance at every stage; Darla Crispin, as I've noted, did much of the preliminary work; Kathleen Snyers managed the production process with her usual skill and good humour. They have collectively corrected as many errors as I could reasonably be expected to generate; if any remain, of course, I claim full responsibility.

William Brooks
University of York, England

REFERENCES

Bartoli, Jean-Pierre, and Jeanne Roudet. 2013. *L'Essor du romantisme: La fantaisie pour clavier de Carl Philipp Emanuel Bach à Franz Liszt.* Paris: Vrin.

Block, Geoffrey, and J. Peter Burkholder, eds. 1996. *Charles Ives and the Classical Tradition.* New Haven, CT: Yale University Press.

Brooks, William. 2007. "Pragmatics of Silence." In *Silence, Music, Silent Music*, edited by Nicky Losseff and Jenny Doctor, 97–126. Aldershot, UK: Ashgate.

———. 2009. "Sounds, Gamuts, Actions: Cage's Pluralist Universe." In *MetaCage: Essays on and around* Freeman Etudes / Fontana Mix / Aria, edited by William Brooks, 61–95. Collected Writings of the Orpheus Institute. Leuven: Leuven University Press.

Crooks, Edward James. 2011. *John Cage's Entanglement with the Ideas of Coomaraswamy.* PhD thesis, University of York (UK).

Dewey, John. 1934. *Art as Experience.* New York: G. P. Putnam's Sons.

Ives, Charles. 1922. *114 Songs.* Redding, CT: C. E. Ives.

———. 1962. *Essays before a Sonata and Other Writings.* Edited by Howard Boatwright. New York: W. W. Norton & Company.

Morgan, Robert. 1997. "'The Things Our Fathers Loved': Charles Ives and the European Tradition." In *Ives Studies*, edited by Philip Lambert, 3–26. Cambridge: Cambridge University Press.

Ribe, Neil, and Friedrich Steinle. 2002. "Exploratory Experimentation: Goethe, Land, and Color Theory." *Physics Today* 55 (7), 43–49.

Steinle, Friedrich. 1997. "Entering New Fields: Exploratory Uses of Experimentation." In "Proceedings of the 1996 Biennial Meetings of the Philosophy of Science Association. Part II: Symposia Papers," supplement, *Philosophy of Science* 64 (December): S65–S74.

PLAYING WITH IMAGES: CHARACTER AND EMOTIONS IN THE AGE OF ROMANTICISM*

Edoardo Torbianelli

SCHOLA CANTORUM BASILIENSIS (BASEL)
AND HOCHSCHULE DER KÜNSTE (BERN)

Recent research has revealed important information concerning traditional Romantic performance practice. Through studying pedagogical sources from the period, much can be learned about pianoforte dynamics, articulation, and accentuation (particularly agogic), as well as the use (or omission) of the sustaining pedal and arpeggiation. Similar insights can be gained about vibrato or the absence thereof, portamenti, and glissandi in singing and on bowed instruments. Fortunately, Romantic performance practice is of increasing interest in professional music schools, with a focus on historical interpretation as well as on modern instrumental training.

To seek authenticity and artistic refinement in this repertoire we should, however, go beyond the rediscovery of simple performance rules. Pedagogical sources and other evidence from the first half of the nineteenth century reveal other, equally important aspects of performance practice. Deep comprehension of any piece requires an understanding of its emotional content. The ability to identify the poetic image from which the composition is taken, the connection between interpretation and emotional experience, and the connection to one's own profound self when performing (by means of concentration or "trance") is fundamental.

These intangible elements are often difficult to grasp; they are nearly ineffable, a challenge to emulate and put into practice. Nevertheless, they are essential to artistic expression and effective Romantic music performance.

---

* Translated by Maria Andrea Parias. Quotations are also translated by Maria Andrea Parias except when attributed to a publication or to Mark Hutchinson (MH).

INDIVIDUAL SENSITIVITY. A CONDITION FOR ARTISTIC PERFORMANCE

Sensitivity to one's feelings is the key to successful artistic interpretation, more than any performance "manner." This is clearly expressed in sources from the early Romantic period and even from the latter part of the eighteenth century. It seems essential to take into account some of the information presented in the *Klavierschule oder Anweisung zum Klavierspielen* of Daniel Gottlob Türk (1789), unquestionably one of the most important reference sources about traditional piano teaching, even during the early 1800s:

> If everything that has been taught in the last two parts is followed in the most meticulous way it is still not possible to have good execution because the most essential part is missing, namely the expression of the prevailing character without which no listener can be moved to any great degree. This effect, which is the highest goal of music, can only be induced when the artist has the capacity to become infused with the predominant affect and to communicate his feelings to others through the eloquence of music. Expression is therefore that part of a good execution in which the true master, full of genuine feeling for his art, distinguishes himself noticeably from the average musician. Mechanical skill can ultimately be learned by much practice; only expression presupposes—other than mechanical facility—a broad range of knowledge, and above all things, a sensitive soul. . . .
>
> The words: will he come soon? can merely through the tone of the speaker receive a quite different meaning. Through them a yearning desire, a vehement impatience, a tender plea, a defiant command, irony, etc., can be expressed. . . . In the same way tones by changes in execution can produce a very different effect. It is therefore extremely necessary to study the expression of feelings and passions in the most careful way, make them one's own, and learn to apply them correctly. (Türk 1982, 337)

This concept recalls a similar statement presented in Georg Friedrich Wolf's instructional work *Unterricht im Clavierspielen*: "Good performance consists in the ability to present the feelings of the composer in their true content. For in every piece of music, even when there is no text, there is an idea. The performer must study this idea and seek to make it tangible to the audience through an appropriate performance" (Wolf [1783] 1807, 84, quoted in Scherer 1989, 52, translated by MH).[1]

Figure 1. Joseph Anton Steffan. Capriccio IV in A major, measures 40–49. © 1999 G. Henle Verlag, München. Reprinted with kind permission

A curious and ambiguous example of a *Gedanke* reflecting some of the characteristics of the imaginary worlds hidden in music material is found in a capriccio written by the Bohemian composer Joseph Anton Steffan.[2] As shown in figure 1, at the end of the exposition of this piece, right where Steffan repeats in diminuendo the closing formula of the coda section, the piece gradually loses strength. Then we find the written indication *pensiere*

1. "Dieser gute Vortrag besteht in der Fertigkeit die Empfindungen des Komponisten nach ihrem wahren Inhalte vorzutragen. Denn in jedem Musikstücke, auch in denen, wo kein Text untergelegt ist, ist ein Gedanke. Diesem muß der Ausüber erforschen, und durch einen richtigen Vortrag den Zuhörern fühlbar zu machen suchen."
2. Steffan was active in Vienna between 1760 and 1790. He taught harpsichord at the imperial court and had a very high reputation as a composer and as a performer. Nonetheless, he is unfairly underestimated today. For more information, see Picton (1989).

significante ("significant thought") in the upper part of the staff, indicating a sudden change. Now the piece regains energy and modulates in a surprisingly courageous way. In other words, the interpreter is confronted with an unexpected impulse that gives a new direction to the piece (Steffan 1971).[3]

In the mid-nineteenth century, the use of expressive techniques to obtain the most satisfactory interpretation of a piece was founded on similar principles. A careful reading of the third part of Carl Czerny's pianoforte method shows that applications of significant expressive effects, such as changes of tempo, are merely consequences and manifestations of particular emotional states.

> Not only every whole piece but also every single part either truly expresses some kind of definite feeling, or at least allows such a feeling to be instilled in it through performance.
>
> These general emotions can be: gentle persuasion; slight doubts or indecisive dithering; tender lamentation; quiet devotion; the transition from a state of agitation to one of rest; reflective or contemplative tranquility; sighs and mourning; the murmuring of a secret; bidding farewell; and countless other situations of this kind.
>
> The player to whom the mechanical difficulties of a piece no longer stand in the way will easily find the passages—often consisting only of a few individual notes—where this kind of feeling was either intended by the *composer* or else can appropriately be expressed. And in such cases a little holding-back (*calando*, *smorzando*, etc.) is also usually advisable, since it would be absurd to rush or push the tempo forward here.
>
> In contrast, other passages can signify: sudden playfulness; hurried or curious questioning; impatience, displeasure and outbursts of anger; firm determination; indignant accusations; exuberance and whimsy; terrified flight; sudden surprise; the transition from a state of rest to one of agitation; etc. In such cases pushing and hurrying the tempo (*accelerando*, *stringendo*, etc.) is natural and fitting. (Czerny [1839] 1991, 24, translated by MH; italics original)[4]

---

3. Recorded on Steffan (2010).
4. "Nicht nur jedes ganze Tonstück, sondern jede einzelne Stelle drückt entweder wirklich irgendeine bestimmte Empfindung aus, oder erlaubt wenigstens, eine

Twenty-two years later, Adolph Kullak re-evaluates Czerny's excerpt in his *Aesthetik des Klavierspiels*, stating: "The enumeration of such real-life events that are reflected in music can never be exhaustive. Czerny is merely giving a few examples. . . . The symbolic power of sounds denotes emotional processes and life events that permit and make desirable either a reduction or an increase in tempo" (Kullak 1861, 316, translated by MH).[5]

Earlier in this text, Kullak also discusses the relation between musical material and inward life (in some cases linking them to formal elements) and the need to explore this: "Accent has given life to musical composition. Clarity, comprehensibility and lucidity are imparted to material that, in its particular sensory duality, besides its formal beauty, also reflects the life of certain conditions of the soul more faithfully than any other. . . . Musical material symbolises the torrent of feeling. . . . In the inner structure of musical works, besides the symbolism of the soul and of the sensual, there lie also so many purely, even tangibly formal elements that these must also be taken into account" (ibid.,

---

solche durch den Vortrag hineinzulegen.

Solche allgemeine Empfindungen können sein: Sanfte Überredung; leise Zweifel, oder unschlüssiges Zaudern; zärtliche Klage; ruhige Hingebung; Übergang aus einem aufgeregten Zustande in einen ruhigen; überlegende oder nachdenkende Ruhe; Seufzer und Trauer; Zulispeln eines Geheimnisses; Abscheidnehmen; und unzählige andere Zustände dieser Art.

Derjeniger Spieler, dem die mechanischen Schwierigkeiten des Tonstücks nicht mehrim Wege stehen, wird leicht diejenigen, (oft nur aus einzelnen Noten bestehenden) Stellenausfinden, wo eine solche Empfindung entweder im Willen des *Compositeurs* lag, oder schicklicherweise ausgedrückt werden kann. Und in solchen Fällen ist ein kleines Zurückhalten (*calando, smorzando, etc.*) meistens wohl angebracht, indem es widersinnig wäre, da ein Drängen und Treiben des Zeitmasses anzuwenden.

Andere Stellen können dagegen andeuten: Plötzliche Munterkeit; eilende oder neugierige Fragen; Ungeduld, Unmuth und ausbrechenden Zorn; kräftigen Entschluss; unwillige Vorwürfe; Übermuth und Laune; furchtsames Entfliehen; plötzliche Überraschung; Übergang aus einem ruhigen Zustand in einen aufgeregten, u.s.w. In solchen Fällen ist das Drängen und Eilen des *Tempo*, (*accelerando, stringendo, etc*:) naturgemäss, und an seinem Platze."

5. "die Aufzählung solcher aus dem Leben such in den Tönen abspiegelnder Vorgänge [kann] nicht erschöpft werden. . . . Czerny giebt nur einige Beispiele. . . . die symbolisirende Kraft der Töne [andeutet] Gefühlsvorgänge und Lebensereignisse, welche auf der einen Seite ein Innehalten der Bewegung, auf der andern ein Beschleunigen derselben gestatten und wünschenswerth machen."

300–302, translated by MH).[6] The essential role of emotions and of life experience in composition and consequently in performance is thus clearly and directly described in these sources.

BEETHOVEN: BETWEEN POETICAL SUGGESTION AND A REPRESENATION OF FREE HUMAN CONCIOUSNESS

It is essential to consider Czerny's instructions in order to attain a convincing performance of Beethoven's music. They clearly show the importance of teaching by means of evocative emotions and images and the relationship of these to sensitivity and inner experiences. Here are some examples taken from Czerny's valuable indications:

> [on the Piano Sonata op. 57] Beethoven . . . may perhaps have been thinking here of sea-waves on a stormy night, with a cry for help ringing out in the distance—this kind of image can always give the player a good idea of the right manner of performance. . . . It is certainly true that Beethoven drew inspiration from similar visions and images, drawn from reading or from his own vivid imagination, in the composition of many of his most beautiful works, and that we will only obtain the true key to his music, and to its execution, through a secure knowledge of these circumstances. (Czerny [1842] 1963, 62, translated by MH and MAP)

> [on the Piano Sonata op. 27 (Adagio)] This movement is highly poetic and yet easy for anyone to grasp. It is a night scene in which the lamenting voice of a spirit sounds from a great distance. (51)

> [on the Piano Sonata op. 106 (Adagio sostenuto)] The wonderful composition . . . that portrays the feelings of the aged master, weighed down in body and spirit, who occasionally remembers better days. (66)

---

6. "Der Accent hat das Tongemälde belebt. Klarheit, Verständigkeit, Übersichtlichkeit sind demjenigen Materiale mitgetheilt worden, welches in seiner specifisch sinnlichen Dualität, außer der Schönheit der Form, auch den Lebensverlauf gewisser Seelenzustände so treu abspiegelt wie kein anderes. . . . Das musikalische Material symbolisirte den Strom des Gefühls. . . . In dem Organismus des Tonwerkes liegt außer der Symbolik des Seelenlebens, des Sinnlichen, rein Formellen, ja plastisch Formellen so viel, daß auch diese Faktoren zu Rathe gezogen werden müssen."

[on the Piano Trio op. 70 no. 1 (Largo)] The character of this *Largo* . . . *is* ghostly and nightmarish, like an apparition from the underworld. It would not be out of place to imagine here the first appearance of the ghost in Hamlet. (98)

[on the Piano Concerto no. 1 op. 15 (Largo)] The character of this beautiful movement, expressed through the purest harmonies as well as through heartfelt melody, is a sacred quieting and exalting of the spirit towards the most noble feelings, which the performer should imagine while playing. (106)

[on the Piano Concerto no. 3 op.37 (Largo)] The whole theme must sound as a distant, sacred and transcendental harmony. (110)

[on the Piano Concerto no.4 op.58 (Andante con moto)] In this movement (which belongs, along with the rest of the concerto, to Beethoven's most beautiful and poetic creations), one cannot help but imagine an ancient scene of dramatic tragedy. (112)

[on the Piano Concerto no.5 op.73 (Adagio poco moto)] When Beethoven wrote this Adagio, he had in mind the religious songs of devout pilgrims, and the execution of this movement must fully express the sacred calm and contemplation which is found in this image. (115)[7]

---

7. "Mag sich Beethoven . . . dabei vielleicht das Wogen des Meeres in stürmischer Nacht gedacht haben, während von Ferne ein Hilferuf ertönt, —immer kann ein solches Bild dem Spieler eine angemessene Idee zum richtigen Vortrag . . . geben. Es ist gewiss, dass Beethoven sich zu vielen seiner schönsten Werke durch ähnliche, aus der Lektüre oder aus der eignen regen Fantasie geschüpfte *Visionen* und Bilder begeisterte, und dass wir den wahren Schlüssel zu seinen *Compositionen* und zu deren Vortrage nur durch die sich're Kenntniss dieser Umstände erhalten würden" (62). "Dieser Satz ist höchst poetisch und dabei für jeden leicht fasslich. Es ist eine Nachtscene, wo aus weiter Ferne eine klagende Geisterstimme ertönt" (51). "das wunderbare Tonstück . . ., das die Gefühle des bejahrten, körperlich und geistig niedergedrückten Meistern schildert, der sich bisweilen einer bessern Zeit erinnert" (66). "Der *Character* dieses . . . *Largo* ist geisterhaft erhauerlich, gleich einer Erscheinung aus der Unterwelt. Nicht unpassend könnte man sich dabei die erste Erscheinung des Geist's im *Hamlet* denken" (99). "Der Character dieses schönen Tonsatzes ist eine heilige, durch die reinstes Harmonieen wie durch gefühlvolle Melodie ausgedrückte Beruhigung und Erhebung des Gemüths zu den edelsten Empfindungen, die dem Spieler beim Vortrage immer vorschweben müssen" (106). "das ganze Thema muss wie eine ferne, heilige und überirrdische Harmonie klingen" (110). "Bei diesem Satze, (der, wie überhaupt das ganze *Concert*, zu Beethovens schönsten und poesiereichsten Schöpfungen gehört,) kann man nicht umhim, sich eine antike dramatisch-tragische Scene zu denken" (112). "Als Beethoven dieses

Figure 2. Anton Reicha, *Vollständiges Lehrbuch der musikalischen Composition* (Reicha 1832, 324)

Adagio schrieb, schwebten ihm die religiösen Gesänge frommer Wallfahrer vor, und der Vortrag dieses Satzes muss völlig die heilige Ruhe und Andacht ausdrücken, die in diesem Bilde liegt" (115).

Also pertinent to this discussion is a note found in the appendix to Czerny's German translation of Anton Reicha's composition method (Reicha 1832). While illustrating the structures of some of the most common compositional genres, Czerny presents a harmonic reduction of the first movement from Beethoven's Piano Sonata, opus 53 (see figure 2). Presented this way, the sonata is transformed from a vibrant and animated piece into a kind of church chorale, filled with nobleness and sweetness.

> In its original form, this is one of Beethoven's most brilliant, virtuosic, and demanding sonatas. Yet if one simply plays through the above reduction at the same tempo, how pure and noble the whole harmonic structure is! Indeed, transcribed appropriately for a choir, it would be ideally suited to a solemn, austerely tranquil hymn. All Beethoven's works rest upon this classical foundation, and we can hardly recommend any more useful exercise for the student than to write out the basic chords for many of his other works in this fashion. (Reicha 1832, 329, translated by MH)[8]

Some decades after Beethoven's death, clarity of "speech" and the evocation of atmospheres and of emotive movements were re-evaluated. Anton Schindler described Beethoven's performing style as having "*the clearest and most intelligible declamation*, one which could perhaps only be observed at such a high level in his compositions" (Marx 1863, 48, translated by MAP and MH).[9] Schindler's description was quoted by Adolph Bernhard Marx in his *Anleitung zum Vortrag Beethovenscher Klavierwerke*, and Marx then offered his own interpretation: "he [Schindler] thus implies that beyond the representation of indefinite sensations

8. "Die vorliegende *Sonate* ist, im *Original*, eine der glänzendsten, brillansten und auch schwierigsten Beethovens. Wen[n] mann dagegen, in demselben Tempo, den obigen genauen Grundriss ruhig durchspielt, wie rein und edel ist der ganze Harmonie-Bau! er könnte sich, gehörig für den Singchor gesetzt, sogar zu einem Ernst ruhigen Kirchensatze vollkommen eignen. Auf diesem klassischen Grunde ruhen Beethovens sämmtliche Werke, und wir können dem Schuler schwerlich etwas Nützlicheres anrathen, als recht viele derselben auf dieser Art in allen ihren Grundaccorden zu Papier zu bringen."

9. "*es war die deutlichste, fasslichste Deklamation*, wie sie in dieser hohen Potenz vielleicht nur aus seinen Werken heraus zu studiren sein dürfte."

and movements of the soul, a conscious spirit, having become certain of its own substance and duty, was able to master those emotions. The senses, the agitated, enigmatic heaving of the soul, were the precondition and foundation: the clear-sighted, decided, and decisive spirit was the final objective" (ibid., 48–49, translated by MAP and MH).[10]

This interesting distinction—between a poetical "reading" and a personal, truly "logical" expressivity in music—does not limit performance to one kind of "prosody," even though it stresses Beethoven's conception of expression, which was the general one at the time. For Beethoven specifically, an attention to prosody was undoubtedly significant; his thinking is recorded, for example, in his annotations to Johann Baptist Cramer's *Piano Studies* (published 1974), used for his nephew's lessons and later copied by Schindler, in which metrical equivalents to poetic feet are applied to musical figurations.[11]

Even more, Marx's comments on Beethoven's performances (and also on his compositions) point out their capacity to reveal, within their structure, some aspects of psychic processes and mental paths involving doubt, vacillation, and continuous digression, out of which, at a certain point, a conscious will chooses a resolution that defines the final direction. This is how, pedagogically, the structural and expressive trademarks of Beethoven's works need to be considered, rather than by imposing external sound models. With this approach, Marx (1863, 14–15, translated by MAP and MH) reveals the ambiguous role of words: on the one hand, they are insufficient "to register the subtle veining of vital flow,"[12] and on the other, they offer the only possible way

10. "so deutet er an, dass über die Vorstellung unbestimmter Sinnes- und Seelenbewegung hinaus . . . [sei] ein bewusster, seines Inhalts und seiner Aufgabe ganz gewiss wordener Geist jener Regungen vollkommen Herr geworden. . . . Der Sinn, das aufgeregte, räthselvolle Wogen der Seele waren Vorbedingung und Grundlage; der hell erkennende, bestimmte und bestimmende Geist war Vollender."

11. To understand the importance of phrasing inspired by elocution to piano pedagogy at that time, one should remember Johann Nepomuk Hummel's method for teaching proper phrasing: the key notes in the musical phrases are marked with signs that indicate greater or lesser intensity of support (see Hummel [1838] 1981, 452).

12. "das feine Geäder der Lebensströmung . . . festzuhalten."

towards a learning process in which "the work of art cannot and must not be transmitted; rather, it must be illuminated from the inside. It should not be offered ready and pre-digested to the performer; his own spirit must be elevated and strengthened so that he can take it in."[13]

One example from the section "Die Spielart für Beethoven" shows the confidence with which Marx alternates between technical indications and the use of strong, evocative images:

> In the Trio (marked "minor") of the Sonata in E-flat major, opus 7, both hands must execute the following figure.

Figure 3. Ludwig van Beethoven, Sonata, op. 7, third movement, trio; from Marx 1863, 41

> This must be done with perfect equality, with a slight swell up to the first note of the third bar before fading away again—this should be repeated once more in the same way, and then Beethoven's own dynamic indications are to be followed. From this point onwards, the second part is clearly outlined on its own; the poet's words "in the murmur of the wind / in the silent night" convey the sense of the whole piece. (Marx 1863, 41–42, translated by MAP and MH)[14]

13. "Das Kunstwerk kann und soll nicht überliefert, sondern von seinem Innern heraus durchleuchtet, es soll nicht für den Darsteller zubereitet und mundrecht gemacht, sondern der Geist des Darstellers soll zu ihm erhoben und für dessen Aufnahme gekräftigt werden."

14. "Im Trio (Minore bezeuchnet) der Es dur-Sonate Op. 7 haben beide Hände folgende Figur auszuführen. Dies muss in vollkommner Gleichmässigkeit geschehn, mit gelindem Anwachsen bis zum ersten Ton des dritten Takts, dann wieder abnehmend—und in gleicher Weise nochmal, dann nach der von Beethoven selbst gegebnen Bezeichnung. Der zweite Theil ergiebt sich hiernach von selbst; für den ganzen Satz könnte des Dichters Wort 'Im Windsgeräusch / In stiller Nacht' sinndeutend sein."

Indeed, the choice of technical solutions depends upon clarity of imagination, and the artistic character of a performance depends on the right degree of variety and flexibility of movement:

> What means are at the player's disposal for this kind of interpretation? To find the answer one must be capable of imagining the movements of an agitated soul. Here there is no indifference or coldness, no standing still or letting go; movement and variety always prevail. . . . These situations are reflected in the motion or temporal continuity of sounds, and in the interplay of alternating degrees of intensity that must always be as clearly present in the player's mind as the keys are to his eyes—or rather to his playing instinct. (ibid., 52, translated by MAP and MH)[15]

BAILLOT'S LEGACY: MUSIC AS A PROCESS OF SELF-KNOWLEDGE

The identification of a musical message with one's personal inner world is one of the key points in the pedagogical approach of the French violinist Pierre Baillot, a leading figure at the Paris Conservatory during the first half of the nineteenth century. Baillot, considered by contemporary critics to be a sublime performer and an artist of great purity and profoundness, and described by one of the authors of the *Revue musicale* of 1831 as the only French violinist that could still be cherished and loved after Paganini had left Paris, is remembered in an obituary in the *Revue et gazette musicale de Paris* (25 September 1842) as "the most accomplished kind of artist in the highest and purest sense of the word".[16] Some of the ideas about sound quality in Baillot's method (1834) reflect his aesthetic preferences and tools: "Let

15. "Welche Mittel stehen nun dem Spieler für solche Darstellung zu Gebote? Wer sich das beantworten will, der vergegenwärtige sich, was im aufgeregten Seelenleben vorgeht. Da is nirgend Gleichgültigkeit und Kälte, nirgend Stehenbleiben und Fallenlassen; durchaus waltet Bewegung und Wechsel. . . . Diese Zustände spiegeln sich in der Bewegung oder Zeitfolge der Töne und in dem Wogenspiel der verschiedenen Stärkegrade, die allesammt dem Geiste des Spielers so klar vorliegen müssen, als die Tasten seinem Aug' oder vielmehr seinem Spiel-Instinkt."

16. "le plus accompli de l'artiste dans la plus haute et la plus noble acception du mot."

those who desire a beautiful quality of tone begin to prepare it by the technical means we have indicated. . . . But let them not seek elsewhere than in their own feelings, which they must draw out from their soul, for it is there that they will find its source" (Baillot 1991, 476).

The "resonance" between the inner self of the composer and that of the performer arises from their shared human nature: "We then feel the necessity . . . to seek the true domain of art not in the unknown, not in material things or the physical effects of nature, but in our own hearts, in moral order, and in feeling—this sweet life of the soul and this inexhaustible source of happiness" (ibid., 10).

On a pedagogical level, this path can be structured in a very organised and refined way, as is the case in Baillot's (ibid., 351) explanation of character and expressive tones in music:

> Character is the general colour given to the expression of the composition. It is chosen by the composer to bring out his intention in a way that will seize the soul of the listener by making him feel the sentiment that the composer wanted to portray. . . . Musical character can be divided into four principal characters which serve as the source of the others, and which correspond naturally to the four ages of life and the general progression of the human soul: 1. simple: naïve; 2. vague: undecided; 3. passionate: dramatic; [and] 4. calm: religious.

Baillot then offers a small anthology of excerpts illustrating the precise application of some of these characters (see figure 4).

Similar teaching methods, which make a fundamental connection between music's emotional character and its technical aspects (rhythm, melody, harmony, figuration, etc.), are found in other didactic texts of the beginning of the nineteenth century. These were probably essential to the process through which expressive meaning was assimilated into various genres of composition. This approach can also be found in some pages from the violin method written by Charles de Bériot (1857, 224–41) and even in Manuel García's singing method. The latter contains an appendix with extended excerpts that illustrate expression in Italian opera, in which indications about emotion and character are found with astonishing frequency (García 1847, 82–105). The different kinds

Figure 4. Baillot, *L'art du violon* ([1834] 2001, 203). Reproduced with the kind authorisation of Anne Fuzeau Productions, www.annefuzeau.com

of emotions explored in this document are presented with exceptional intensity and variety of nuance. (Jeanne Roudet explores further implications of García's examples in chapter 3, below.)

Returning to Baillot's violin method, the sublime artist is defined as one who has examined his inner world and used the wisdom arising from his personal life experience. This is the central assertion of the passionate conclusion of this work:

> Happy is he to whom nature has given a profound sensitivity! He possesses within himself an inexhaustible source of expression. The years only increase his richness of expression: they give him new sensations; they vary his situation, they modify his feelings. The more his ideas ripen, the more his reason is enlightened and the more simplicity he acquires in the technique and energy in his effects. Expression for him has crossed the boundaries of art; it becomes, so to speak, the story of his life; he sings of his memories, his sorrows, the pleasures he has tasted, the hurts he has endured. What would only destroy a common talent, he turns to the profit of his art; chagrin sharpens his sensitivity and lends to his *accents* the delicious charm of melancholy. The very trials of adversity, reawakening his energy, exalt his imagination and give him those sublime emotions, those strong ideas born of great obstacles and seeming to spring from the heart of storms. Finally, whatever the destiny that calls him, melody is his interpreter, his faithful friend; it gives him the purest of all enjoyments by revealing to him the secret of communicating the full range of emotions he has, and the secret of enabling his fellow men to become passionately involved in his destiny. (Baillot 1991, 480; italics original)

LISZT AND CHOPIN: SPEAKING SOULS

During the 1830s and 1840s, Paris discovered two other exceptional musicians—performers, creators, and teachers. Their compositions and the way they performed them were described at the time as being remarkably innovative, leaving a profound mark on musical culture. Even if their perceptions are quite distant from one another, Franz Liszt and Frédéric Chopin offered their listeners musical performances well beyond the commercial entertainments and aesthetic pleasantries of most of their contemporaries.

Testimonies about their teaching and performance are relatively abundant. Mme Boissier's diary (published 1927) is particularly significant since she recorded the events that took place during the piano lessons Franz Liszt gave her fifteen-year-old daughter in Paris in 1832. Her writing describes how the great Hungarian virtuoso managed to bring together his inner world with his playing and how he communicated his own strategies to obtain the best possible instrumental and musical development from his students. Liszt apparently revealed his own way of expressing himself through the piano, willingly neglecting differences in talent and skill between himself and his pupils. His method, reflected in a precise and powerful technical and mechanical practice, did not neglect the construction of a solid, intimate structure built on personal awareness of feelings, a refined organisation of mental images and real-life experience. Simplicity, true feeling, and self-awareness are the principal rules: "He is the enemy of affected, stilted, contorted expressions. Most of all, he wants truth in musical sentiment, and so he makes a psychological study of his emotions in order to convey them as they are" (Liszt 1973, xii). "His expression is never pretentious or mundane; it is the reflection of his soul . . .; it is the revelation of all his thoughts and the solace of his heart, with no other purpose than to pour out his noble and burning impressions" (xiv). "One must express only what one feels, and that is where he sees the whole secret of musical expression" (xvii). "We spoke about naturalness in music. I told him that it seemed to me the highest degree in art. He agreed; one must say neither more nor less in music, for one must depict one's heart and nature after having observed them well" (xix). Exercises intended to develop dynamic control must not be "mechanical study, for the soul must always try to express itself" (xiii). "Every musical expression was motivated, studied and reflected upon" (xiii).

The reproduction of passions and real emotions follows the laws of nature and of true, interior human processes. Personal inspiration draws upon meditation, but also from real and profound life experiences:

> [H]e aims at reproducing the strong and true emotions . . . terror, fright, horror, exasperation, despair, love brought to delirium; after these stormy movements come discouragement, weariness, languor, a kind of tranquillity full of softness, of abandonment, of weakness . . . Sometimes, at the height of the tempest an opening appears, one of those corners of "celestial blue" which can be seen at times amidst the darkest clouds. It is a divine melody . . . Then the violence of the passion reappears and sweeps everything along with it . . . To interpret in this manner, one must have seen and felt much, and so, therefore, Liszt seeks emotions eagerly. He struggles with a suffering nature and so he analyzes the language of all pains. He visits hospitals, gambling casinos, asylums for the insane. He goes down into the dungeons, and he has even seen those condemned to die! He is a young man who thinks a great deal, who dreams, who excuses everything; . . . would he not have been a skilled musician, he would have been a philosopher, or a distinguished literary figure. (Liszt 1973, xvi)

Such an approach to music has an educational and edifying impact on those who practise or observe it: "His course of musical declamation could serve, when essential, to cleanse the heart and to elevate all sentiments" (xxiv). "This ability of his to imprint on the keyboard, as on a canvas or a discourse, all passions—their full play, their development, their contrast—constitutes an almost psychological study which perfects talent" (xxv).

Mme Boissier also provides examples of the emotional preparation for some of the pieces studied by her daughter: "Then he played an exercise by Moscheles. . . . Before asking Valérie to start this exercise, he read Hugo's *Ode to Jenny*; through this, he wanted to make her understand the spirit of the composition which he found to have a certain analogy with the poem" (xiii). "He had her play one of Kalkbrenner's exercises. It is a sweet, vague, tender, vaporous exercise, and I compared it to a beautiful, but slightly hazy, autumn morning. 'You should say spring morning,' said Liszt, with a smile" (xiii).

In two different lessons, the Minuetto from Carl Maria von Weber's Sonata no. 4 in E minor, opus 70, is mentioned: "It is a wild, surprising and wonderful composition. It begins with zest, fire, energy, in an uproar; then, suddenly, the trio begins. It is a waltz and he interprets it innocently, vaguely. A lone dissonance thrown in the midst of this tender, soft music is present like a bad thought . . ." (Liszt 1973, xiv). "This minuet depicts perfectly the madness, the wandering, the disruptiveness, the incoherence of an upset mind. One must play in this manner, interrupting the phrases, introducing agitation, the disorder of insanity, of an insanity which sometimes reaches a furious despair; then comes the trio, similar to a lucid recovery, to a light joy . . ." (xvi).

Finally, the diary reveals Liszt's ideas about the relationship between emotions and musical structure, accomplished at the very moment of the creative act: "There are, in the passages which he improvises, harmonic detours, modulations in minor intersected with the melody that create a charming effect. They are like reflections or melancholy thoughts in the midst of cheerful events; they are like clouds that for a short while pass in front of the sun and hide its brilliance" (Liszt 1973, xxii).

Despite the enormous difference in style and inspiration between Liszt's and Chopin's music,[17] it is possible to identify parallels and similarities in testimonies about the teachings of Liszt and of the Polish genius. Moreover, Liszt's performing style and Chopin's playing share an essential and important trait: beyond all specific sounds, dynamics or agogic details, they are reflections of the performers' souls, characterised by true expression and a capacity to lead a listener into a parallel dimension.

This is what the Marquis de Custine writes in two letters addressed to Chopin: "I rediscovered you and with you the piano, without its tiresome features, without its meaningless notes, but with the thoughts that you express in spite of the instrument itself. You do not play on the piano but on the human soul. . . . You have gained in suffering and poetry; the melancholy of your composition penetrates still deeper into one's heart; one is alone with you in the midst of a crowd; it is not a piano that speaks

---

17. "Chopin, the aristocrat, was a pianist *da camera*; Liszt, the eloquent tribune, was a man of the stage. Chopin brought to the piano the refined art of *bel canto*; from the same piano Liszt wrenched sonorities evoking Berlioz or Wagner. While the Pole's aesthetic is based on the voice, the Hungarian's is inspired by the orchestra" (Eigeldinger 1986, 20).

but a soul, and what a soul!" (Eigeldinger 1986, 286). Then, from Baron de Trémont's testimony: "In effect, what one hears is no piano; it is a succession of fresh touching thoughts, often melancholy, sometimes tinged with terror; and to convey them the instrument undergoes a thousand transformations under his fingers . . ." (286). Anton Schindler declared that "The prime virtue of this great master of the keyboard lies in the complete *truth of expression of every feeling* . . ." (292, italics original).

German pianist and conductor Carl Hallé recorded in his autobiography his impressions of Chopin's performance in November 1836 at one of Baron Eichtal's salons: "The same evening I heard him play, and was fascinated beyond all expression. It seemed to me as if I had got into another world . . . I sat entranced, filled with wonderment . . . In listening to him you lost all power of analysis; you did not for a moment think how perfect was his execution of this or that difficulty; you listened, as it were, to the improvisation of a poem, and were under the charm as long as it lasted" (Eigeldinger 1986, 271). Even Robert Schumann agrees about the remarkable concentration evident in Chopin's performances: "It was already an unforgettable picture to see him sitting at the piano like a clairvoyant, lost in his dreams . . ." (269).

Moreover, for Chopin, acquiring a penetrating understanding of a musical piece is linked to the evocation of images and the development of a psychological analysis. In discussing Chopin's approach to teaching his nocturne, op. 15 no. 3, Jan Kleczyński confirms the composer's desire that understanding be individual and distinctive, though grounded in an image: "It was originally intended to be called 'After a representation of the tragedy of *Hamlet*'. Afterwards Chopin abandoned this notion, saying: 'Let them guess for themselves'" (Eigeldinger 1986, 79). Another illustration is found in a letter written by the composer during his early years, in which he speaks about the slow movement of his Concerto in E minor: "The *Adagio* [*sic*] of my new *Concerto* is in E major. . . . giving the impression of someone looking gently towards a spot which calls to mind a thousand happy memories. It is a kind of reverie in the moonlight on a beautiful spring evening" (67).

More images appear in Wilhelm von Lenz's suggestive remarks on some of Chopin's pieces:

> [on the Mazurka op. 17 no. 4] Even in Chopin's presence we called it "the mourner's face" [*das Trauergesicht*]—he was quite happy about this name. (Eigeldinger 1986, 74)
>
> [on the Mazurka op. 30 no.3] "It seems like a Polonaise for a coronation festivity," said someone to Chopin. "Something like that," was his reply. (75)
>
> [on the Nocturne op. 48 no. 2] When Gutmann studied [this] Nocturne with Chopin, the master told him that the middle section (the *più lento* in D flat major) [bars 57–100] should be played as a recitative. "A tyrant commands" (the first two chords), he said, "and the other asks for mercy." (81)
>
> [on the Scherzo op. 31 (bars 1–2)] "It must be a question . . . It must be a house of the dead . . ." (84–85)

According to Karol Mikuli, "Any work selected for study should be carefully analysed for its formal structure, as well as for the feelings and psychological processes which it evokes" (Eigeldinger 1986, 59). The expressive conceptions in Chopin's music, at least as defined and described by direct witnesses, seem to continually oscillate between poetry and prose, elocution and lyricism, manifestation of emotion and thought, nature and refinement. The definitions of musical art sketched by Chopin in his draft *Esquisses pour une méthode de piano* clearly reflect a conception of the link between sound and thought that reconnects with aesthetic attitudes of the Classic and late Baroque periods: "The expression of our perceptions through sounds. The expression of thought through sounds. The manifestation of our feelings through sounds" (Eigeldinger 1986, 195).

Even those who had no direct contact with Chopin's teachings or performances, but who possessed a profound sensitivity and a superior technique, were capable of coming very close to emulating Chopin's playing, to the point of being able to identify themselves with it. It is to this that Wilhelm von Lenz refers, in his well-known recollections of virtuoso piano players, when speaking about the famed Carl Tausig. Having heard Tausig play two of Chopin's compositions (the Nocturne in C minor, op. 48 no. 1, and the Barcarole, op. 60), Lenz (who had met, followed, and received lessons from Chopin in Paris in 1842) described Tausig as remarkably like Chopin and writes that ". . . in the Barcarole, Tausig was the living impersonator of Chopin. He felt as he did, he played like him, he *was* Chopin at the piano!" (Lenz [1971] 1983, 71).

Chopin himself was surprised by how his young pupil Carl Filtsch (a pianistic genius who died prematurely in 1845 at the age of fifteen) performed his compositions with absolute comprehension of their expressive message, despite a distinct difference in character and before having heard them played by the composer or having received advice from him: "Never has anybody understood me like this child, the most extraordinary I have ever encountered. It's not imitation, it's an identical feeling, instinct, which makes him play without thinking, with all simplicity as if it could not be any other way. He plays me almost all my own compositions without having heard me, without my showing him the least thing—not completely like me (for he has his own style) but certainly no less well" (Eigeldinger 1986, 142). The composer gave Filtsch complete freedom of interpretation: "We each understand this differently, but go your own way, do as you feel, it can also be played like that" (13). This valuable statement reveals Chopin's view about freedom of interpretation: a performer does not have to play exactly as the master; his interpretation can also be valuable and artistically acceptable even if it is slightly different, as long as it contains the intimate essence of the composition.

The secret of one possible connection between a composer and an interpreter lies in comprehending the poetry within a specific piece. This was suggested to von Lenz by Tausig himself before playing the *Barcarole*. His explanation enabled von Lenz to understand the piece: "This tells . . . of two persons; of a love scene in a secret gondola—we might even call it symbolic of lovers' meetings in general. That is expressed in the thirds and sixths. The dual character of two notes—or two persons—runs through the whole; it is all two voiced, or two souled. In the modulation into C sharp major (marked 'dolce sfogato'), you can recognise a kiss and an embrace—that is plain enough" (Lenz [1971] 1983, 71). Shortly afterwards, after playing a four-hand Schumann composition with von Lenz, Tausig exclaimed, "You play that exactly as *he* would!" Von Lenz answered, "But there is not much to play . . . only to understand"; and Tausig replied with humour, "That is just it—you can't teach that to your lady pupils!" (78).

At this point it is appropriate to mention the statements Adelina de Lara (1872–1961) made during a radio interview in 1949. On that occasion she described the teaching methods of and the instructions received from her illustrious teacher Clara Wieck Schumann, with whom she studied at the Conservatory of Frankfurt between 1886 and 1891:

> One of the strongest impressions Clara Schumann's teaching left on my mind is that of her intolerance of affectation and sentimentality. I'm not referring to true expression, for no one felt music more keenly than she did. She taught us to play with truth, sincerity, and love, to choose music we could reverence, not just music which merely displayed one's technique. We were told to be truthful to the composer's meaning, to discover and emphasise every beauty in the composition, to see pictures as we played. "A real artist must have vision," she said. If the music were to mean anything to our listeners, it must mean even more to us, and in giving pleasure to our hearers we had a great purpose to fulfil. (De Lara 1949, 0:51)

The ability to associate images with music when performing appears to be one of the most important qualities for an artist-performer to develop, together with discovering all the hidden beauties of a piece, with love and sincerity. The importance of images does not eliminate the need for skill in the more concrete parameters of expression (later in the interview De Lara confirms this, noting the careful attention Clara Schumann gave all technical matters, such as tone quality, rhythm, and phrasing); but it appears to be clear that it is mostly the force of imagination that allows us to make aesthetic choices and that this force manifests itself and becomes intelligible through the application of a performer's technique.

I believe there is still much work to be done to reconstruct the different levels of expression of Romantic music, to individualise the roles of the components in each message, and to integrate these elements and reveal them to our listeners. Performers who seek true stylistic authenticity in their performances must understand the importance of sharing not only their intellects but also their entire inner selves.

Even on a pedagogical level—entirely apart from technical matters and the relationship between technique and artistic expression—discussion with students concerning stylistic authenticity and related topics should not be limited to the "tip of the iceberg," the "rules of declamation" in the eighteenth-century tradition. It must also encourage a brave and generous personal involvement from the performer. The poetical analysis of compositions, an intuitive suggestion of images capable of illuminating the meaning of some passages, a profound study of expressive subtleties through observing the affective life of human beings—all of these should play an important part in every music lesson, even more within specialised programmes of study devoted to early music performance. This is why it is necessary to assimilate and reapply all aspects of Romantic expression seriously and creatively. The contemporary performer and teacher of Romantic music must be able to evoke and live with suggestive images that are spontaneously related to the music, to be aligned with the attitudes of the time rather than merely implementing diligently expressive effects borrowed from a treatise.

There is still room to deepen our understanding of the relationship between affective context and compositional structures by following historical documentation and, through research and analysis of individual experiences, by internalising the emotional contents typical either of a particular historical and cultural context or simply present in every individual, separate from any specific context. Most of all, we should not forget that music is intended to have an extraordinary effect on those who practise it and on those who listen. Without this purpose and without this faith, the true objective of making music will be missed.

REFERENCES

Bériot, Charles de. 1857. *Méthode de violon*. Paris: Schott.

Baillot, Pierre Marie François de Sales. 1834. *L'Art du Violon: Nouvelle méthode*. Paris: Dépot central de la musique. Reprinted in facsimile as Baillot (1834) 2001. Translated by Louise Goldberg as Baillot 1991.

———. (1834) 2001. *Violon: Les grandes méthodes romantiques de violon; Vol. 3, Baillot: L'art du violon: Nouvelle méthode dédiée à ses élèves*. Realised by Nicolas Fromageot. Méthodes et traités, Série 2, France 1800–1860. Courlay: Fuzeau. Facsimile reprint of Baillot 1834.

———. 1991. *The Art of the Violin*. Edited and translated by Louise Goldberg. Evanston, IL: Northwestern University Press. First published as Baillot 1834.

Boissier, Auguste, Mme. 1927. *Liszt Pédagogue: Leçons de piano données par Liszt à Mademoiselle Valérie Boissier à Paris en 1832*. Paris: Honoré Champion. Translated by Elyse Mach in Liszt 1973, ix–xxvi.

Cramer, Johann Baptist. 1974. *21 Etüden für Klavier nach dem Handexemplar Beethovens aus dem Besitz Anton Schindlers*. Edited by Hans Kann. Vienna: Universal Edition.

Czerny, Carl. (1839) 1991. *Von dem Vortrage: (1839): Dritter Teil aus* Vollständige theoretisch-practische Pianoforte-Schule, *op. 500*. Edited by Ulrich Mahlert. Wiesbaden: Breitkopf & Härtel. Czerny's *Pianoforte-Schule* first published 1839 (Vienna: Diabelli).

———. (1842) 1963. *Über den richtigen Vortrag der sämtlichen Beethoven'schen Klavierwerke: Czerny's "Erinnerungen an Beethoven" sowie das 2. und 3. Kapitel des IV. Bandes der Vollstandigen theoretisch-practischen Pianoforte-Schule, op.500*. Edited with a commentary by Paul Badura-Skoda (Vienna: Universal). Partial facsimile reprint of *Die Kunst des Vortrags der ältern und neuen Claviercompositionen, oder Die Fortschritte biz sur neuesten Zeit: Supplement (oder 4ter Theil) zur grossen Pianoforte-Schule von Carl Czerny, op.500, in 4 Capiteln* (Vienna: Diabelli, 1842). Also contains "Erinnerungen an Beethoven (Auszug)," (manuscript, written 1842), and "Anekdoten und Notizen über Beethoven" (manuscript, written 1852).

De Lara, Adelina. 1949. "Clara Schumann and Her Teaching" (radio interview). On *Pupils of Clara Schumann*, Adelina De Lara, Ilona Eibenschütz, and Fanny Davies (pianists), CD 2, track 1. Pearl, GEMM CDS 99049, 1991, 6 compact discs.

Eigeldinger, Jean-Jacques. 1986. *Chopin: Pianist and Teacher as Seen by His Pupils*. Edited by Roy Howat. Translated by Naomi Shohet with Krysia Osostowicz and Roy Howat. Cambridge: Cambridge University Press. First published 1970 as *Chopin vu par ses élèves: Textes recueillis, traduits et commentés* (Neuchâtel: La Baconnière); English edition translated from the 2nd ed. (Neuchâtel: La Baconnière, 1979).

García, Manuel Patricio Rodríguez. 1847. *Traité complet de l'art du chant*. Paris: E. Troupenas et Cie. First published 1840–47 (Paris: Schott).

G[uéroult], A[dolphe]. 1842. 25 September. "Baillot." *Revue et gazette musicale de Paris* 9 (39): [385]–387.

Hummel, Johann Nepomuk. (1838) 1981. *Méthode complète théorique et pratique pour le Piano-forte*. Geneva: Minkoff. First published 1828 as *Ausführliche theoretisch practische Answeisung zum Pianofortespiel* (Vienna: Haslinger); 2nd ed. published 1838 (Vienna: Haslinger). Translated into English as *A Complete Theoretical and Practical Course of Instructions, on the Art of Playing the Piano Forte* (London: T. Boosey, 1828). This edition based on the French translation by Daniel Jelensperger (Paris: A. Farrenc, 1829).

Kullak, Adolph. 1861. *Die Ästhetik des Klavierspiels*. Berlin: Guttentag.

Lenz, Wihelm von. (1971) 1983. *The Great Piano Virtuosos of Our Time*. Translated by Madeleine R. Baker. Translation revised and edited by Philip Reder. London: Kahn & Averill. This edition first published 1971 (London: Regency Press). Baker's translation first published in English as *The Great Piano Virtuosos of Our Time, from Personal Acquaintance: Liszt, Chopin, Tausig, Henselt* (New York: Schirmer, 1899). Originally published 1872 as *Die großen Pianoforte-Virtuosen unserer Zeit aus persönlicher Bekanntschaft* (Berlin: B. Behr's Buchhandlung [E. Bock]).

Liszt, Franz. 1973. *The Liszt Studies . . . Including the First English Edition of the Legendary Liszt Pedagogue*. Edited and translated by Elyse Mach. New York: Associated Music Publishers. *The Legendary Liszt Pedagogue* first published as Boissier 1927.

Marx, Adolph Bernhard. 1863. *Anleitung zum Vortrag Beethovenscher Klavierwerke*. Berlin: Otto Janke.

Picton, Howard. 1989. *The Life and Works of Joseph Anton Steffan (1726–1797): With Special Reference to His Keyboard Concertos*. New York: Garland.

Reicha, Anton. 1832. *Vollständiges Lehrbuch der musikalischen Composition*. Translated and annotated by Carl Czerny. 4 vols. Vienna: Diabelli. Vol. 1 first published as *Cours de composition musicale, ou Traité complet et raisonné d'harmonie pratique* (Paris: Gambaro, ?1816–18); vol. 2 first published as *Traité de mélodie* (Paris: Scherff, 1814); vols. 3–4 first published as *Traité de haute composition musicale* (Paris: Zetter, 1824–26).

Scherer, Wolfgang. 1989. *Klavier-Spiele: Die Psychotechnik der Klaviere im 18. und 19. Jahrhundert*. Munich: W. Fink.

Steffan, Joseph Anton. 1971. *Capricci*. Edited by Alexander Weinmann. Fingerings by Hans-Martin Theopold. Munich: G. Henle.

———. 2010. *Works for Pianoforte*. Performed by Edoardo Torbianelli (fortepiano). Pan Classics, PC 10219, 2 compact discs.

Türk, Daniel Gottlob. 1789. *Klavierschule oder Anweisung zum Klavierspielen für Lehrer und Lernende mit kritischen Anmerkungen*. Leipzig: Schwickert; Halle: Hemmerde und Schwetschke. Republished in facsimile, edited by Siegbert Rampe (Kassel: Bärenreiter, 1997). Translated by Raymond H. Haggh as Türk 1982.

———. 1982. *School of Clavier Playing; or, Instructions in Playing the Clavier for Teachers and Students*. Translated by Raymond H. Haggh. Lincoln, NE: University of Nebraska Press. First published as Türk 1789.

Wolf, Georg Friederich. (1783) 1807. *Unterricht im Klavierspielen*. 5th ed. Halle: Johann Christian Hendel. First published 1783 (Göttingen: Grape).

"INNER VOICES" AND "DEEP COMBINATIONS"
ROBERT SCHUMANN'S APPROACH TO ROMANTIC POLYPHONY

Hubert Moßburger

STAATLICHE HOCHSCHULE FÜR MUSIK
UND DARSTELLENDE KUNST STUTTGART

E. T. A. Hoffmann's famous definition of romantic music is a statement about so-called absolute music:

> [Instrumental music] is the most romantic of all arts, one might almost say the only one that is genuinely romantic, since its only subject-matter is infinity. . . . Music reveals to man an unknown realm, a world quite separate from the outer sensual world surrounding him, a world in which he leaves behind all precise feelings in order to embrace an inexpressible longing. (Hoffmann 1989, 96)[1]

In contrast, vocal music cannot reach this "inexpressible longing," because words give determinate meaning to the music. For Hoffmann it is Beethoven who is "a purely romantic composer," and so it is no wonder that this composer is not successful in "vocal music, since it does not permit a mood of vague yearning but can only depict from the realm of the infinite those feelings capable of being described in words" (ibid., 98).[2]

On the other hand, the Romantic generation required the union of the different arts, as was captured in Friedrich Schlegel's phrase "progressive universal poetry" (*progressive Universalposie*) (Schlegel 1968, 140).[3] From this perspective the art song, as a

---

1. "Sie [die Instrumentalmusik] ist die romantischste aller Künste, beinahe möchte man sagen, allein echt romantisch, denn nur das Unendliche ist ihr Vorwurf. . . . Die Musik schließt dem Menschen ein unbekanntes Reich auf, eine Welt, die nichts gemein hat mit der äußeren Sinnenwelt, die ihn umgibt und in der er alle *bestimmten* Gefühle zurücklässt, um sich einer unaussprechlichen Sehnsucht hinzugeben" (Hoffmann [1810–14] 1993, 26–27).
2. "Vokalmusik, die den Charakter des unbestimmten Sehnens nicht zulässt, sondern nur durch Worte bestimmte Affekte, als in dem Reiche des Unendlichen empfunden, darstellt, weniger gelingt" (Hoffmann [1810–14] 1993, 29).
3. Schlegel's phrase first appeared in a fragment in the *Athenaeum*, commonly cited as fragment 116 (Schlegel 1798, 28).

combination of poem and music, would seem to be an ideal realisation of Romantic aesthetics. But how to connect these two different manifestations of "inexpressible longing"—"infinite" instrumental music on the one hand, and vocal music with "precise" words on the other? It was Felix Mendelssohn Bartholdy who found an ingenious solution: his "songs without words" are wholly instrumental music, but with a texture of exposed melody and accompaniment they imply a singing voice. Conversely, with the integration of the singing voice into the piano part, Robert Schumann created a level of art song to which the idea of absolute music contributed. In 1843, Schumann made his views explicit:

> Paralleling the development of poetry, the Franz Schubert epoch has already been followed by a new one which has utilized the improvements of the simultaneously developed instrument of accompaniment, the piano. . . . The voice alone cannot reproduce everything or produce every effect; together with the expression of the whole the inner details of the poem should also be emphasized; and all is well so long as the vocal line is not sacrificed. (R. Schumann 1946, 75)[4]

Mendelssohn's instrumental songs and Schumann's vocal instrumentals are both attempts to dissolve the limits of the art form in pursuit of "inexpressible longing." And both have a missing link that intensifies this Romantic desire, an "infinite" element that can only be intuited by suggestion and fantasy: in Mendelssohn's piano pieces the words are missing, and in Schumann's songs or instrumental works sometimes a consistent melody must be found or completed by the listener.

The absence of both—words *and* melody—is evident in Schumann's postlude to the song cycle *Frauenliebe und Leben*, op. 42:

4. "Im Zusammenhange mit der fortschreitenden Dichtkunst ist der Franz Schubert'schen Epoche bereits eine neue gefolgt, die sich namentlich auch die Fortschritte des einstweilen weiter ausgebildeten Begleitungsinstruments, des Klaviers, zu Nutze machte. . . . Die Singstimme allein kann allerdings nicht alles wirken, nicht alles wiedergeben; neben dem Ausdrucke des Ganzen sollen auch die feineren Züge des Gedichts hervortreten, und so ist's recht, wenn darunter nicht der Gesang leidet" (R. Schumann 1843, 120).

Figure 1. Robert Schumann, *Frauenliebe und Leben*, op. 42, no. 8, bars 28–37

The descending melodic phrase in the upper part in bars 31–32 recurs inconspicuously in the middle voices of the following bars. The upper voice stagnates into a repeated pitch and longer durations. From bar 34 the impression is more of a figured chorale or polyphonic harmony than of a single, melody-dominated texture. The intention of this fragment is revealed by a comparison with the first song:

Figure 2. Robert Schumann, *Frauenliebe und Leben*, op. 42, no. 1, bars 8–15

The accompaniment in these bars is identical to the piano postlude of the last song. The singing voice in the first two-bar phrase is in unison with the upper voice of the piano. In the following bars (from bar 10), the singing voice is distinct from the accompaniment, though doubled by a middle voice in the piano. Schumann's use of the accompaniment in the postlude sounds clearly as a repetition of the first song. At the moment when the melody is hidden the listener remembers the singing voice and the text of the first song, especially the very characteristic and expressive phrase in bar 12 ("taucht aus tiefstem Dunkel"). We reflexively complete the melodic gap in the postlude (b. 35) with the singing voice we remember from the first song (b. 12).

The postlude is not only a memory of the first song but also a reflection upon the last words in the last song (Schumann [1890], 105, my translation):

> Ich zieh' mich in mein Inn'res still zurück,
> der Schleier fällt,
> da hab' ich dich und mein verlornes Glück,
> du meine Welt!
>
> I withdraw into my inner self quietly,
> the veil falls;
> there I have you and my lost happiness,
> you, my world!

The absent words and the hidden melody in the postlude may be a symbol of the widow's lost happiness and of her retreat into an inner world (see Rosen 1995, 112–15; Muxfeldt 2001). She cloisters herself away; she leaves behind Hoffmann's "outer sensual world" ("äußere Sinnenwelt"), with all its "precise feelings" ("bestimmte Gefühle").

"INNER VOICES"

The relationship between the "outer sensual world" and the absence of an exposed melody gives rise to an aesthetic and technical concept that Schumann called the "inner voice" (*innere Stimme*).[5] Beside its metaphorical connotations of intuition and inspiration, the adjective *inner* can be interpreted in two ways. First, it can be understood as the musical space that is enclosed by the outer voices; from this point of view, the inner voice is one of the middle parts. In the example from Schumann's *Frauenliebe und Leben*, the singing voice, which is transferred in the postlude to an instrumental part, withdraws from an exposed, outer voice into an inner one—just as, psychologically, the widow withdraws into her "inner self" after her husband has died. Second, the inner voice can be understood perceptually as a non-existent voice that nonetheless arises inside the player or the listener (similarly to the acoustic effect of difference or combination tones, which are perceived but not notated). Schumann heard it in more complicated or polyphonic textures, where it can stay secret and subtle, only shimmering through: "How a secret melody shimmers even in Bach's most artfully convoluted works, as it does in all of Beethoven's" (R. Schumann 1841, [1]; my translation).[6]

Let me illustrate this esoteric idea by tracing how music that is outward and explicit is transferred to an inner voice. I shall start with the following melody:

Figure 3. The outward basis for an "inner voice"

This chorale-like melody can be harmonised in four parts in a simple way, with diatonic triads and a Phrygian cadence at the end (see the upper row of chord notation in figure 3). Compared with this, Schumann's harmonisation (the lower row) is more

5. The phrase appears explicitly in the score to *Humoreske*, op. 20, discussed below.
6. "Wie schimmert doch selbst in den kunstvollst verschlungenen Gebilden Sebastian Bachs eine geheime Melodie hindurch, wie in allen Beethovens."

advanced: the falling diatonic fifths become secondary seventh chords, and E♭ major is varied by the minor. But in Schumann's original composition, the *Humoreske*, op. 20, the melody is doubly hidden. Temporally the cantus firmus is overstretched to four-bar phrases, and spatially it is distributed among different voices (figure 4):

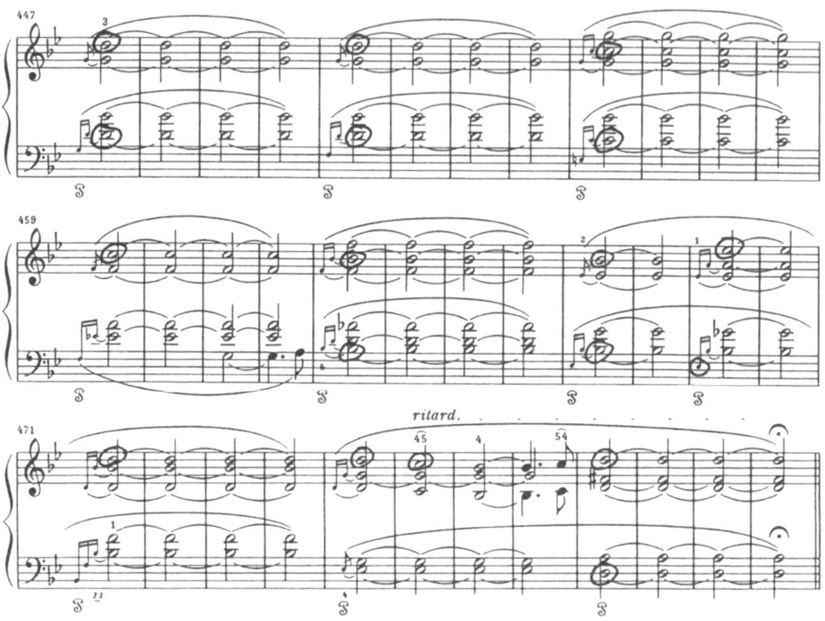

Figure 4. The melody in Schumann's *Humoreske*, op. 20, bars 447–82

The loss of metre, time, and one-dimensional linear construction destroys the coherence of the melody; the line is absorbed into the harmonic space. When the personal "inner voice" is not revealed by the composer, it is impossible to guess; other lines might also be extracted and sung from the chords. This is an important consideration: the inner voice is very individual and open in its interpretation. If we are to see the composer's own inner ear or heart, this voice must be made evident. This Romantic paradox—in which interior, hidden material is nonetheless expressed—was famously depicted earlier in the *Humoreske* (figure 5):

Figure 5. The "inner voice" in Schumann's *Humoreske*, op. 20, mm. 251–58

The "virtual," unplayed voice is notated on a third system between the outer, "real" parts. The harmony is played as a fast dance-like accompaniment in the lower system, and the inner voice results from the latent polyphony in the embellished upper part. Schumann has marked the main tones with double stems at the beginning of every bar. The only exception is the E♭ in the fifth bar of the example. This is not simply a personal intervention by the composer but also a necessary melodic extension to the otherwise unsounded melody.

For Clara Schumann, the inner voice here is meant to be an indication of the melody that is in the right hand. She has two explanations for dealing with this inner voice, which should not be played by the piano:

> I think that the composer, in a fantastic way, wanted the melody more to be intuited than accentuated. But it could also be supposed that my husband meant only that the player should think of the voice inwardly

> or should hum it, as often happens when one is wholeheartedly absorbed in playing. (C. Schumann quoted in Appel 2005, 1:113, my translation)[7]

This places the inner voice as the highest expression of interiority and subjectivity in a Romantic aesthetic: the melody should not be accentuated or loudly and clearly presented; it is more intuitive and fantastical, something only to be thought or hummed to oneself. The composer himself also spoke about this kind of unconscious singing: "Who of us in the twilight hour has not sat at his upright piano . . . and in the midst of improvising has not unconsciously begun to sing a quiet melody?" (R. Schumann 1946, 210).[8]

"DEEP COMBINATIONS"

The adjective *inner* is related to *deep*, which has a qualitative and a spatial meaning. As opposites of *superficial* and in their connotation of concealment both adjectives—*inner* and *deep*—are aesthetic synonyms. Schumann's second phrase, "deep combinations," implies a concern with craftsmanship: how to compose or combine musical materials in a deep way. This can be realised horizontally in relations between the motifs and vertically through counterpoint or harmony. Schumann states that the "deep combinations" in the music of his contemporaries have their source mostly in Bach: "The [deep] combinations, the poetry and humor of modern music, originate chiefly in Bach"

7. "Der Componist hat, glaube ich, in phantastischer Weise die Melodie mehr ahnen lassen wollen, als sie etwa gar markiert, hervorgehoben zu wissen. Es ist aber auch anzunehmen, daß mein Mann sich nichts weiter dabei gedacht, als daß der Spieler sich innerlich die Stimme denkt oder mitsummt, so wie man es ja öfter thut, wenn Einem das Herz recht voll ist beim Spielen." From a letter to Georg Henschel, London, 14 May 1883.

8. "Wer hätte nicht einmal in der Dämmerungsstunde am Klavier gesessen . . . und mitten im Phantasieren sich unbewusst eine leise Melodie dazu gesungen?" (R. Schumann 1835, 202). In a letter to Clara, 4 January 1838, Robert imagines a scene with her: "I'll improvise for you at twilight, and sometimes you will sing along softly" (Schumann and Schumann 1984–87, 1:71). ("Abends phantasire ich Dir in der Dämmerung vor und Du wirst dazu manchmal leise singen" [Schumann and Schumann 1984–2001, 1:71].) In the twentieth century, Glenn Gould has discovered many "inner voices" in all kinds of piano music.

(1946, 93, translation modified).[9] In another quotation he makes his meaning clearer:

> We know all about Bach and other artists of intricate combination—artists who, from a few bars, often mere notes, built wonderfully interconnected pieces, throughout which the opening lines are threaded in countless plaits; artists whose inner ears were so admirably keen that the extremes of their art can only be perceived with the help of the eye. (R. Schumann 1842, 178; my translation)[10]

An economical use of notes as the basic material for building wonderful pieces is a prime technical aspect of deep combination. A modern term for this is Hans Mersmann's "shared substance" (Substanzgemeinschaft) (see Appel 1981, 81). *Deep* corresponds with *substance* and *combination* with *shared*:

Deep Combination = Shared Substance

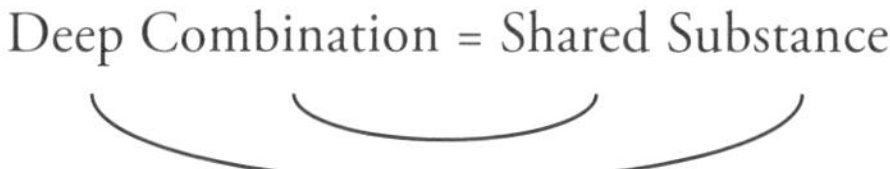

The more economical the musical material, the more you can feel the substance and the unity. The classic technique for developing substance is to work with motifs and themes. But unlike Beethoven, Schumann tends to hide his substance, to leave it underground. In the "Sphinxes" of his *Carnaval*, op. 9, the composer only reveals the substance in the middle of the cycle, in the famous coded motifs "Es–C–H–A" (E♭–C–B–A), "As–C–H" (A♭–C–B), and "A–Es–C–H" (A–E♭–C–B). Moreover, Schumann does not develop his material in a clear or logical way. In his early works, in particular, material is developed more through an associative procedure of variation, with the "foundations" of the

9. "Das Tiefcombinatorische, Poetische und Humoristische der neueren Musik hat seinen Ursprung aber zumeist in Bach" (R. Schumann 1887, 1:221).

10. "Wir wissen wohl von Bach und andern verwickelt kombinierenden Künstlern, wie sie auf wenige Takte, oft Noten ganz wundersam gefügte Stücke gegründet, durch die sich jene Anfangslinien in unzähligen Verschlingungen hindurchziehen, von Künstlern, deren inneres Ohr so bewundernswürdig fein schuf, daß das Äußere die Kunst erst mit Hilfe des Auges gewahr wird."

construction hidden; "the combinations ought to be only accidental," as Schumann put it (1946, 79).[11]

There is also an interesting parallel between the term *shared substance* and the unity of the different arts called for by the Romantic generation. Schumann's highest aesthetic value is placed on the poetic (das Poetische), which is defined as the common substance of the different arts:

---

technique: shared substance
aesthetic: common substance of the arts

"Associative magic" (Beziehungszauber)—Thomas Mann's term for pervasive motivic unity—operates horizontally or formally, unfolding through time. But a second aspect of Schumann's understanding of the "deep combination" is found in counterpoint. In the quotation above, Schumann (1842, 178) speaks about "countless plaits" of voices. At other places he calls such passages "bravely labyrinthine" (kühn labyrinthischen) or "wonderful in the interlocking of tones" (wunderbares in der Verflechtung der Töne) (R. Schumann 1838c, 98; 1834, 1:402; my translation). This calls to mind E. T. A. Hoffmann's (1989) descriptions of counterpoint, which draw on German Romantic images from nature: "wonderful contrapuntal intricacies" (99); "mysterious combinations" that are compared to "wonderfully interwoven mosses, herbs and flowers" (94); and "labyrinthine pathways of some fantastic park, hedged in by all kinds of rare trees, shrubs, and exotic flowers" (100).[12] When exploring these mysterious and wonderful braids of voices, it is not possible to perceive all the subtleties of the polyphonic deep combinations—particularly the "inner

11. "Das Combinatorische darf nur das Zufällige sein" (R. Schumann 1904, 388). Letter to Ludwig Meinardus, December 28, 1853.

12. "wunderbare kontrapunktische Verschlingungen"; "geheimnisvolle Kombinationen . . . wunderlich verschlungenen Moosen, Kräutern und Blumen"; "mit allerlei seltenen Bäumen, Gewächsen und wunderbaren Blumen umflochtenen Irrgärten eines phantastischen Parks" (Hoffmann [1810–14] 1993, 32, 24, 33).

voices"—except with the help of the eyes. This kind of hidden counterpoint is the technique for creating Romantic polyphony. And the ideal vehicles for composing "deep combinations" and hidden counterpoint in textures are the inner voices. So both terms—*inner voice* and *deep combination*—are two sides of the same coin, Schumann's Romantic polyphony:

---

inner voice(s) → Romantic polyphony ← deep combination(s)

Schumann combined the idea of the "inner voice" and of the "deep combination" in the motto, taken from Friedrich Schlegel's "Die Gebüsche" (Schlegel 1962, 191), that preceded his Fantasy in C Major, op. 17 (translation from Rosen 1995, 101):

> Durch alle Töne tönet
> Im bunten Erdentraum
> Ein leiser Ton gezogen
> Für den der heimlich lauschet.
>
> Through all the sounds that sound
> In the many-colored dream of earth
> A soft sound comes forth
> For the one who listens in secret.

The "soft sound" is the inner voice, and it "comes forth" in a kind of development as a secret or inner melodic thread that creates thematic unity (see R. Schumann 1914, 1:409, 2:112). And the shared substance of this "deep combination" is a musical quotation from "Nimm sie hin denn, diese Lieder," from Beethoven's song cycle *An die ferne Geliebte*, op. 98 (here, of course, addressed to Clara Wieck). Both the soft and the emerging sound are composed unconsciously ("in the many-colored dream of earth") and will be received secretly ("for the one who listens in secret"). Thus the motto of Schlegel sounds as an instruction or a guide for the listeners and players of Schumann's Romantic polyphony.

Composition with "deep combinations" and "inner voices"

After this first theoretical approach to the two basic ideas of Schumann's special kind of Romantic polyphony, we have now to ask how it works in his compositions. It is true that Schumann relates his idea of "deep combinations" to the music of Bach, but this is only a starting point: to imitate the pure canons or fugues of Bach's work would result—in Schumann's scathing terms—merely in a "philistine accentuation of the entries of the fugue subject" (R. Schumann 1946, 89).[13] Neither Baroque contrapuntal art nor the thematic workings of the Classical style can form the basis of Romantic polyphony. In order to achieve his goal, Schumann has to find other approaches. This new polyphony requires a changed role for the melody and a new treatment of voice leading. Schumann responded to these requirements by emphasising the interior of the texture and by neutralising the conventional idea of the contrapuntal voice. These two techniques create closer interconnections between the individual parts of the composition and strengthen the whole to form a deep combination.

Emphasising the interior of the texture

If a polyphonic texture is to be "deep" or "inwardly focussed," this cannot happen at the surface. As a critic, Schumann often looked at the middle voice as an important criterion of a good composition. For himself he declared: "I often take such odd middle parts which are characteristic of me" (Schumann and Schumann 1984–87, 1:50).[14] In Schumann's early piano music, indeed, the middle voices are often made somewhat polyphonic. We can see this clearly when a passage is compared with its sketches (figures 6 and 7):

13. "philiströses Merkenlassen des eintretenden Themas" (R. Schumann 1838b, 22).
14. "ich nehme oft so curiose Mittelstimmen, woran ich zu erkennen bin" (Schumann and Schumann 1984–2001, 1:51). Letter to Clara Wieck, 29 November 1837.

Figure 6. Robert Schumann, sketch, *Papillons*, op. 2, no. 1, mm. 3–8 (Gertler 1931, 145)

Figure 7. Robert Schumann, published version, *Papillons*, op. 2, no. 1, mm. 3–8

In bars 4–7 Schumann derives a countermelody to the main melody in the upper voice. This lower part is not the bass but a tenor *cantilena*. It is created from the bass and the tenor of the chords in the sketch. So Schumann converts an inner voice from the accompaniment into a new contrapuntal line. The stereotyped waltz accompaniment of the sketch is broken up for a deeper, more interconnected texture.

Another technique for concentrating on the interior of the texture is to place the main voice in the middle part. We saw it in the withdrawal of the vocal line in the postlude of Schumann's *Frauenliebe und Leben*, and we can hear it in the fifth song, "Ich will meine Seele tauchen," from *Dichterliebe*, op. 48, where the singing voice is enclosed by the piano accompaniment like the calyx of a lily, out of which Heinrich Heine's text speaks. Another interesting middle line can be seen in the F♯-major Romance, op. 28, no. 2:

Figure 8. Robert Schumann, Romance, op. 28, no. 2, mm. 1–3

As in the *Humoreske*, there is a middle system here, where the main voice is placed. But this "inner voice" is real, not imaginary; it is "inner" only in spatial terms. The tenor is accompanied by the upper bass in parallel thirds. These two middle voices, which come out of the broken chords, sound like mirrored projections around a shared centre. This spatial internalisation could be understood as a musical expression of Schumann's introverted character. And this concentration on an inner core, a stable centre, avoids the extremities, difficulties, and superficial effects of the virtuoso composers whom Schumann combated as a critic.

Neutralising the conventional idea of the contrapuntal voice

If a texture is to be "inward" and "deep" in a polyphonic way, the conventional idea of the contrapuntal voice as a closed, one-dimensional, simply accompanied line must be dissolved. This can be accomplished in three stages: first, the "verticalisation" of parts (parallel voices and imprecise unisons); second, the intertwining of voices (splitting voices, crossing voices, breaking up of voices [stimmige Brechung],[15] and complementary voices); and third, the creation of imaginary voices.

Verticalisation causes two voices to become one. Intertwining—for example, splitting voices or crossing voices, which both produce similar effects—leaves the listener unable to identify the voice leading. Only the eye can tell which is which. In a diary entry from September 1839, Clara Wieck noted that quality in Robert's music: "His compositions are all orchestral in conception, and I believe that is why the public understands them so little, because melodies and figures so cross one another that it requires much training to find out their beauties" (Litzmann 1913, 256).[16]

15. This term is taken from Jacob Gottfried Weber (1824, 1:157). It is simply a latent polyphony that arises from "the representation of many parts by a single one" (Vorspiegeln mehrere Stimmen durch eine) (ibid; translation from Weber 1851, 136).
16. "Seine Compositionen sind alle orchestermäßig, und ich glaube, daher dem Publicum so unverständlich, indem sich die Melodien und Figuren so durchkreuzen, daß viel dazu gehört, um die Schönheiten herauszufinden" (Litzmann 1902, 373).

Such indifference to distinctions of register creates in the listener that "beautiful confusion," which was prized in early Romantic musical aesthetics as an expression of humour or irony. This happens, for example, in the first two bars of "Ende vom Lied," the last piece in Schumann's *Fantasiestücke*, op. 12 (figure 9):

Figure 9. Robert Schumann, "Ende vom Lied," *Fantasiestücke*, op. 12, no. 8, bars 1–2

The right hand has to play a combination of voice splitting and voice crossing. Attempts to follow the individual parts will lead only to confusion, because they merge into one another, creating a series of bell-like sounds. Acknowledging this confusion, the pianist has to play the passage "with a good sense of humour" ("Mit gutem Humor") as Schumann requires in his expression mark. The end of the song leads to an unexpected, mysterious coda with extended chord-repetitions in dotted values like a funeral march (figure 10).

The "bell theme" in bars 101–10 sounds in augmented values as an echo in the upper and middle voices before withdrawing into the tonic. This seems to be the real "end of the song": the melody, which is the essential carrier of a song, is dissolved into sound. All suggestions of the instrumental singing voice are lost in the space containing only an F major chord circling around itself. The combination of the funeral-march rhythm with the "bell theme" evoked for Schumann the simultaneous pealing of wedding and funeral bells. On 17 March 1838, he wrote to Clara Wieck: "I was thinking at the time, 'Well, everything will end with a merry wedding'—but towards the end my sorrow over you

Figure 10. Robert Schumann, "Ende vom Lied," Coda

returned, and so it sounds like a combination of wedding bells and death knells" (Schumann and Schumann 1984–87, 1:124).[17]

After verticalisation and the intertwining of voices, the last stage in hiding a melody is to compose it as an imaginary voice.[18] As the manner of suggestion becomes increasingly subtle, culminating in the total concealment of the melody, increasing levels of imagination are required. The techniques used are broken chords, embedded melodies, subtractive melodies, and remembered melodies. Embedded melody we have seen in the *Humoreske* (figure 4); a subtractive melody is created by taking notes away successively from a chord as a negative arpeggio—for example, at the end of *Papillons*, op. 2, or in the first version of

17. "ich dachte dabei, nun, am Ende löst sich doch Alles in eine lustige Hochzeit auf—aber am Schluß kam wieder der Schmerz um Dich dazu und da klingt es wie Hochzeit- und Sterbegeläute untereinander" (Schumann and Schumann 1984–2001, 1:121).
18. All these techniques are described in Moßburger (2005, 66–90).

the *Abegg-Variationen*, op. 1 (Finale, bars 197–98); and a remembered melody we have seen in the postlude of *Frauenliebe und Leben* (figure 1), where there is just the accompaniment and the listener remembers the melody that was heard before (another example is the end of the first version of the Impromptus, op. 5). It only remains to examine potential Romantic polyphony in broken chords.

Unlike broken voices, discussed above, the outline of melodies in broken chords is secondary. Broken harmony is more important than broken melody here. Only the upper notes of the chords can be noticed as melodic lines. But if a composer wants to hide inner voices, this kind of texture is ideal to submerge them in "the bottomless sea of harmony," as Richard Wagner put it (1900, 285).[19] And the lines in this inner area are open to interpretation; their perception depends upon individual imagination. Diverse melodic lines can be traced in the "Kleine Studie" from the *Album für die Jugend*, op. 68, no. 14 (figure 11); and they enable us, perhaps, to discover the composer's hidden intention.

Figure 11. Robert Schumann, "Kleine Studie," op. 68, no. 14, bars 1–4

First we hear the upper notes B–C–E–D emerge from this wavelike motion over a pedal point. This line is set against the tetrachord D–E–F♯–G in the upper voice of the left hand; together they form a reasonable two-part-texture. But there is also another, more esoteric voice: the middle part of the left hand, B–C–C–B, is neither characteristic nor conspicuous; but when taken in conjunction with the gestural movement of the

19. "das bodenlose Meer der Harmonie" (Wagner 1869, 264).

whole texture, Schumann's "little study"[20] hints at the model of "big brother" Bach's famous C-major Prelude, which has an identical upper voice:

Figure 12. Johann Sebastian Bach, Prelude in C major, BWV 846, bars 1–4

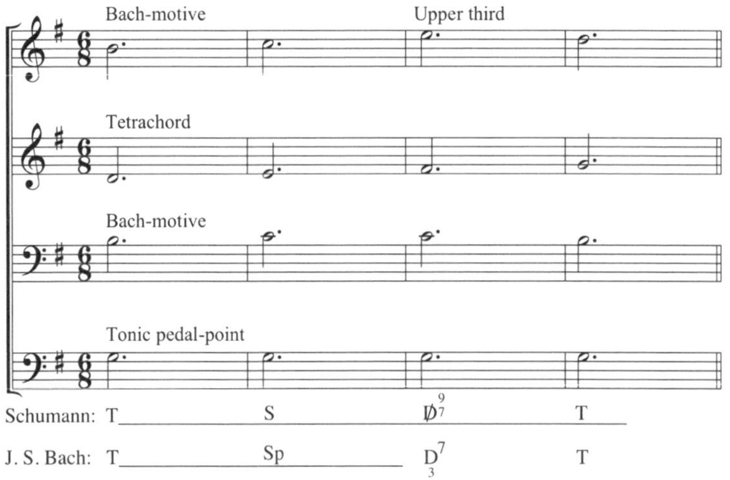

Figure 13. Motives and harmony (Schumann and Bach)

20. Schumann advised a young composer to look in Bach's *Wohltemperiertes Klavier* "so that he could get to know more chords" (Schumann 1837, 39; my translation; damit er mehr Accorde kennen lerne). In comparison to Bach's C-major Prelude, Schumann's piece could also be called a "little chordal study," introducing the youth to different kinds of chords (eight different chords, compared with six different chords in Bach's Prelude).

This quotation from Bach's upper part, which is hidden by Schumann as an "inner voice," takes on a personal inflection in its third bar: after it has been doubled by the upper part in bars 1–2, Schumann sets the third (E) over C, thus obtaining a harmony that is different from Bach's $^{6}_{5}$ chord: it is a half-diminished seventh chord over the pedal point. This chord is rarely used as a substitute dominant in the Baroque period; its inclusion of elements of tonic, subdominant, and dominant functions gives it a more Romantic, shimmering quality. The Baroque quotation is coloured with a modern sound. Later, in bars 44–49, the more concrete musical cipher B♭–A–C–H is woven in different voices of the harmony. In a chapter titled "Suspending the Difference between Melody and Accompaniment" (Aufhebung der Unterscheidung von Melodie und Begleitung) from the *Große Kompositionslehre*, Hugo Riemann (1902, 239, my translation) distinguishes an "unaccompanied figured melody" (begleitungslos figurierte Melodie) from an "accompaniment without melody" (melodielose Begleitung). Riemann quotes Schumann's "Kleine Studie" as an example of the latter category. For Riemann this evokes organic metaphors similar to "florid counterpoint," but within a Romantic context: "the melody only shimmers like flower buds out of the tips of this accompanimental ornamentation" (ibid).[21]

Should the pianist now underline some specific "inner voices"? Surely not: this would contradict the intention of Romantic polyphony, which should be ambiguous, open, and intuitive. A direct presentation of one of the inner voices of the chords, in the manner of Charles Gounod's adaptation of Bach's C-major Prelude, would have been dismissed by Schumann as superficial or philistine. But the pianist and the informed listener should know the possibilities of the hidden lines. After an analytical, structurally lucid performance has been achieved, there must follow a second level that gives Romantic unconscious perception a chance. With a nod to Hegel ([1813] 1834, 111), who

21. "die Melodie schimmert nur wie Blütenknospen aus den Spitzen dieses begleitungsartigen Rankenwerks."

speaks of a second (zweite) or mediated immediacy (vermittelte Unmittelbarkeit), I will call this *the second indeterminacy of the inner voices*. And now Schumann's expression mark "to be played softly and very evenly" (Leise und sehr egal zu spielen) takes on a deeper meaning: when this instruction is obeyed, listeners are free to develop their own fantasies, but at the same time their subconscious can draw upon the previously analysed possibilities of Romantic polyphony. So the best way to keep the appearance of immediacy, and to play the "Kleine Studie" according to authentic historic performance practice, is to follow Clara Schumann's opinion (quoted above) that an "inner voice" should be more an intuition than an accentuation.

CONCLUSION

The preceding analysis of some of Schumann's instrumental works approached Romantic polyphony as the subject of perceptual and performing possibilities between imagination and realisation. The "inner voice(s)" and their deep combinations create an integrative melodic texture that intensifies the interdependency of the individual parts. And it intensifies the imaginative power of the listeners. Melodic hints, which in the most extreme case leave a gap that must be filled by the imagination, involve the listener in the composition not only as a passive but as an active partner. In contrast to a strict polyphonic fugue, in which the listener is directed by individual consistent lines, hidden counterpoint stimulates the imagination to create its own new secret melodic threads. The freedom which is thus found in Romantic polyphony points towards the concept of the open work in twentieth-century music, where the interpreter can create the composition or parts of it independently.

Schumann's instrumentalisation of melody in the context of "deep combinations" has a specific Romantic meaning. Here, vocality and instrumentality coincide with the "inner voice," presented "ohne Worte." As explained above, Schumann destroyed the fixed voices of earlier polyphony to obtain instrumental fragments for a new kind of polyphony. But the listener has still a desire for traditional melody. Following the psychological law of proximity, we try to hear a consistent melodic line out of the "deep combinations" of polyphony. The line is hidden as an inner voice that can be imagined and sung or hummed as Clara and Robert Schumann did. This is a very Romantic attitude: it seems as if the outer, lost melody will be found again—deep inside.

REFERENCES

Appel, Bernard R. 1981. *Robert Schumanns Humoreske für Klavier op. 20: Zum musikalischen Humor in der ersten Hälfte des 19. Jahrhunderts unter besonderer Berücksichtigung des Formproblems.* PhD Thesis, Universität des Saarlandes.

———. 2005. "Humoreske op. 20." In *Robert Schumann: Interpretationen seiner Werke*, edited by Helmut Loos, 2 vols., 1:113–13. Laaber: Laaber-Verlag.

Gertler, Wolfgang. 1931. *Robert Schumann in seinen frühen Klavierwerken.* Berlin: Georg Kallmeyer.

Hegel, Georg Wilhelm Friedrich. (1813) 1834. *Wissenschaft der Logik. Erster Teil: Die Objective Logik. Zweite Abteilung: Die Lehre vom Wesen.* Edited by Leopold von Henning. Berlin: Dunder und Humblot. First published 1813 (Nuremberg: Schrag).

Hoffmann, E. T. A. (1810–14) 1993. *Kreisleriana.* Edited by Hanne Castein. Stuttgart: Reclam. *Kreisleriana* first published 1810–14 as a series of individual text in various periodicals, principally *Allgemeine musikalische Zeitung*; republished in Hoffmann's *Fantasiestücke in Callot's Manier* (Bamberg: Kunz, 1814–15). Castein's edition first published 1983 (Stuttgart: Reclam).

———. 1989. *E. T. A. Hoffmann's Musical Writings:* Kreisleriana, The Poet and the Composers, *Music Criticism.* Edited by David Charlton. Translated by Martyn Clark. Cambridge: Cambridge University Press. For further bibliographic details on *Kreisleriana*, see Hoffmann (1810–14) 1993.

Litzmann, Berthold. 1902. *Clara Schumann: Ein Künstlerleben.* Vol. 1, *Mädchenjahre, 1819–1840.* Leipzig: Breitkopf und Härtel. Translated by Grace E. Hadow as Litzmann 1913.

———. 1913. *Clara Schumann: An Artist's Life.* Vol. 1. Translated and abridged from the fourth edition by Grace E. Hadow. London: Macmillan & Co. First published as Litzmann 1902.

Moßburger, Hubert. 2005. *Poetische Harmonik in der Musik Robert Schumanns*. Sinzig, Germany: Studio.

Muxfeldt, Kristina. 2001. "*Frauenliebe und Leben* Now and Then." *19th-Century Music* 25 (1): 27–48.

Riemann, Hugo. 1902. *Der homophone Satz*. Vol. 1 of *Große Kompositionslehre*. Berlin: W. Spemann, 1902–13.

Rosen, Charles. 1995. *The Romantic Generation*. Cambridge, MA: Harvard University Press.

Schlegel, Friedrich. 1798. "Fragmente." *Athenaeum* 1 (2): [3]–146.

———. 1962. *Kritische Friedrich-Schlegel-Ausgabe*. Edited by Ernst Behler. Vol. 5, *Dichtungen*, edited by Hans Eichner. München: Verlag Ferdinand Schöningh.

———. 1968. *Dialogue on Poetry and Literary Aphorisms*. Translated, introduced, and annotated by Ernst Behler and Roman Struc. University Park, PA: The Pennsylvania State University Press. Includes a translation of Schlegel 1798.

Schumann, Clara, and Robert Schumann. 1984–2001. *Briefwechsel. Kritische Gesamtausgabe*. 3 vols. Edited by Eva Weissweiler and Susanna Ludwig. Frankfurt am Main: Stoemfeld/Roter Stern. Vols. 1–2 translated as Schumann and Schumann, 1984–87.

Schumann, Clara, and Robert Schumann. 1984–87. *The Complete Correspondence of Clara and Robert Schumann. Critical Edition*. 2 vols. Edited by Eva Weissweiler. Translated by Hildegard Fritsch and Ronald L. Crawford. New York: Peter Lang.

Schumann, Robert. 1834. "Bach." In *Damen Conversations Lexicon*, edited by Carl Herloßsohn, 10 vols., 1:402–3. Leipzig: Volckmar. Reprinted in R. Schumann 1914, 2:200–01.

———. 1835. "Felix Mendelssohn, sechs Lieder ohne Worte für das Pianoforte." *Neue Zeitschrift für Musik* 2 (50): 202. Reprinted in R. Schumann 1914, 1:98–99.

———. 1837. "Etuden für das Pianoforte." *Neue Zeitschrift für Musik* 7 (10): 39. Reprinted in R. Schumann 1914, 1:286.

———. 1838b. "Carl Czerny, die Schule des Fugenspiels." *Neue Zeitschrift für Musik* 8 (6): [21]–22. Reprinted in R. Schumann 1914, 1:[353]–54.

———. 1838c. "Adolph Henselt, zwölf Etuden." *Neue Zeitschrift für Musik* 8 (25): [97]–98. Reprinted in R. Schumann 1914, 1:354–58.

———. 1841. "Kirchenmusik. Eduard Sobolewsky: 'der Erlöser.'" *Neue Zeitschrift für Musik* 15 (1): [1]–2. Reprinted in R. Schumann 1914, 2:7–10.

———. 1842. "Drei Preissonaten." *Neue Zeitschrift für Musik* 16 (1): [177]–79. Reprinted in R. Schumann 1914, 2:79–83.

———. 1843. "Lieder und Gesänge." *Neue Zeitschrift für Musik* 18 (30): 120–21. Reprinted in R. Schumann 1914, 2:[123]–24.

———. 1887. *Robert Schumanns Leben aus seinen Briefen*. Edited by Hermann Erler. 2 vols. Berlin: Ries & Erler.

———. [1890]. *Sämtliche Lieder für eine Singstimme mit Klavierbegleitung*. Vol. 1. Revised by Max Friedlaender. Leipzig: C. F. Peters.

———. 1904. *Robert Schumanns Briefe*. Edited by F. Gustav Jansen. 2nd ed. Leipzig: Breitkopf und Härtel. 1st ed. published 1886 (Leipzig: Breitkopf und Härtel).

———. 1914. *Gesammelte Schriften über Musik und Musiker*. Edited by Martin Kreisig. 5th ed. 2 vols. Leipzig: Breitkopf und Härtel. 1st ed. published 1854 (Leipzig: Wigand).

———. 1946. *On Music and Musicians*. Edited by Karl Wolff; translated by Paul Rosenfeld. New York: Pantheon. First published 1854 as *Gesammelte Schriften über Musik und Musiker* (Leipzig: Wigand).

Wagner, Richard. 1869. *Oper und Drama*. 2nd ed. Leipzig: J. J. Weber. Translated as Wagner 1900.

———. 1900. *Opera and Drama. Richard Wagner's Prose Works*. Vol. 2. Translated by William Ashton Ellis. 2nd ed. London: Kegan Paul, Trench, Trübner & Co. 1st edition published 1893.

Weber, Jacob Gottfried. 1824. *Versuch einer geordneten Theorie der Tonsetzkunst*. 4 vols. 2nd ed. Mainz: B. Schotts Söhne. Translated as Weber 1851.

———. 1851. *The Theory of Musical Composition*. Translated by James F. Warner; edited by John Bishop. 2 vols. London: Robert Cocks and Co. First published as Weber 1824.

FREDERIC CHOPIN, CLARA SCHUMANN, AND THE SINGING PIANO SCHOOL

Jeanne Roudet

UNIVERSITÉ PARIS-SORBONNE

In the nineteenth century, treatises generally asserted that the human voice was the best possible model for instrumentalists and that their art could be appraised by the way they could *sing* with their instruments. Such statements became a cliché of music teaching, and they convey little more than a hazy meaning today. The situation was quite different in Chopin's day, when all the models were to be found in the vocality of the time.

Many sources highlight the affinities between Chopin and Clara Schumann. Information about Chopin is diverse and extensive; concerning Clara Wieck Schumann, a primary source is the treatise her father devoted to piano playing and the art of singing, *Clavier und Gesang* (Wieck 1853).[1] Like Chopin, Clara Schumann was a great teacher—she taught and trained pupils in the Frankfurt Conservatory from 1878 to her death. Thus we also have several documents and recordings (some made as late as the 1950s) that testify first-hand to her teaching. These various sources show that what Chopin and Clara Schumann actually have in common is a concept of singing and that it is this that shapes the similarities in their piano styles—as virtuosi, as composers, and as teachers. These similarities also define their common opposition to another style of piano playing, which, in brief, is embodied by Franz Liszt. Consequently, I will later turn to Liszt to discover what this clear-cut contrast can teach us about Chopin and Clara Schumann's "singing piano" school.[2]

1. Translated as *Piano and Song (Didactic and Polemical)* (Wieck 1988).
2. The present article draws on the results of work that is not specific to piano and on productive links drawn between the study of written sources from the nineteenth century and recorded evidence from the early twentieth century (see in particular, Steane 1974; Crutchfield 1990a, 1990b; Philip 1992, 2004; Brown 1999; Milsom 2003; Hamilton 2008a; Leech-Wilkinson 2009; Peres da Costa 2012; Toft 2013).

A MUTUAL ADMIRATION

I would like to start by briefly mentioning some biographical details. As an eleven-year-old girl, Clara Wieck discovered Chopin through the enthusiasm Robert Schumann expressed in his article about Chopin's Variations on "Là ci darem la mano." She was also guided by the professional judgement of Friedrich Wieck, her sole teacher. He made her practise this work, and it quickly became part of her repertoire. This marked the beginning of a long career dedicated to composers very dear to her: Chopin, Mendelssohn, Schumann, and, later, Brahms.

At the end of 1835, Chopin visited Friedrich Wieck in Leipzig and listened to Clara for the first time. In a letter dated 6 February 1836, Thérèse Wodzinska reported that Chopin had cried while hearing her play (Chopin 1953–60, 2:173 [letter 194]). In March 1839, Chopin himself wrote to Julian Fontana, "You are right to like Clara Wieck's playing; it is very good" (ibid., 2:316 [letter 300], my translation).[3] Though this seems a slight remark, it must be remembered that Chopin very rarely complimented his fellow pianists on their playing. All these incidents, taken together, suggest an artistic affinity between the two pianists.

A COMMON AESTHETIC BASE

The Clavichord

Before discussing vocality itself, it must be noted that Chopin and Clara Wieck grew up in a part of Europe where Viennese instruments were played. The instruments built in the years 1820–30 were the rightful heirs to the pianos played by Mozart thirty years before. They were strongly connected to the clavichord, a fashionable instrument in German-speaking countries in the eighteenth century. In that region, even as the piano was being developed, that other struck-string instrument remained long favoured by the *Kenner* (connoisseurs) and was considered

3. "Tu as raison d'aimer le jeu de Clara Wieck; il est fort bon."

to be the best keyboard instrument to study because it required a very precise touch. Mendelssohn, whom Wieck called an "ideal artist-virtuoso," practised on a Silbermann clavichord until his death (Wieck 1988, 149; see also Hamilton 2008b, 23).

The Viennese piano

The Viennese maker Conrad Graf, who made the piano Clara got for her wedding, built instruments that allowed the pianist to perform very fine articulations, punctuating musical phrases as in Mozart's time. This characteristic of Viennese instruments explains Chopin's well-known preference for Pleyel's pianos (see Eigeldinger 2004, 2010), which were most like the Viennese models among the pianos that could be found in Paris when Chopin settled there. An early account of Viennese instruments was published by Andreas Streicher in 1801. I will summarise here his assertions (see Streicher 1801, 14–28):

1. A Viennese piano must be played with a precise and varied touch so that all its rich sound possibilities will be explored.
2. A precise touch is also required for long notes because the dampers are very efficient.
3. This instrument can't bear being played with arm weight and muscular strength.
4. Nevertheless this instrument provides a bright tone. To play in a brilliant way, one must quickly strike the keys and make them bounce, by playing chords in arpeggio, for instance.

Johann Nepomuk Hummel (1778–1837): the brilliant style and the cantabile

At the beginning of the nineteenth century, Hummel was the pianist who most truly embodied a Viennese aesthetic. Celebrated as a model of pianistic perfection, he developed a cantabile art that had its roots in the Italian bel canto tradition. He also devised a virtuosic way of writing that perfectly matched the precision of Viennese instruments.[4]

Chopin's Variations on "Là ci darem la mano" show that he had completely assimilated Hummel's pianistic style (see Kroll 2007). Chopin played the variations for the first time in Vienna on a piano built by Graf. The instrument's precision was perfectly suited to the brilliant style of the variations. In the 1830s, "brilliant style" evoked a pianistic aesthetic that is rather difficult to grasp; Fétis gave some clues, especially in the text he wrote for the *Méthode des Méthodes*. The "brilliant style" is a synthetic style that reached its peak in the 1830s. More than a school, it was connected to personalities, namely Hummel and Moscheles. It must be remembered that, when the Conservatory of Leipzig was established, Mendelssohn asked Moscheles to teach piano after Wieck refused. I am particularly interested in one aspect of Fétis's definition: this brilliant style is characterised by "mannerisms of production"—that is, an extremely varied tone palette.

> The legato, even and refined playing of the schools of Clementi and Kalkbrenner is remarkable for a great mechanical correctness and for its elegant ease. All is beautiful, pure, regular in the classic examples of these schools. They don't allow what I will call mannerisms of production, mannerisms that I find in Hummel's school, and even more in that of Moscheles. The latter calls for striking the notes in different ways according to the desired effect, and everybody asserts that these special artistic resources are not used in vain, and that his touch is as remarkable for its variety as for its brilliance. (Fétis and Moscheles 1840, 3, my translation)[5]

4. A comparison with Beethoven's playing is revealing, as is the Viennese preference for Hummel (see Czerny [1842] 1968, 1956).
5. "Le jeu lié, égal et poli de l'école de Clementi et de celle de Kalkbrenner est remarquable par une grande correction de mécanisme, et par son élégante facilité. Tout est beau, pur, régulier, dans les types de ces écoles. On n'y admet pas ce que j'appellerai les procédés de production, procédés que je trouve dans l'école de Hummel, et encore plus celle de Moscheles. Celui-ci a plusieurs manières différentes d'attaquer la note, en raison de l'effet qu'il veut produire, et tout le monde avoue que ce n'est point en vain qu'il fait usage de ces ressources d'un art particulier, et que son jeu est aussi remarquable par la variété que par le brillant."

The same processes were used by Chopin and Clara, processes they both had inherited from the Viennese piano technique and the Italian singing school.

CLAVIER UND GESANG: A CONTROVERSY AROUND TWO DIFFERENT CONCEPTIONS OF SINGING AND PLAYING

Chopin and Clara shared a love of bel canto. They studied it before recommending it to their students. Chopin discovered it in Warsaw; and Clara was in good hands, since her father was a renowned piano and singing teacher, as much respected in one field as in the other. In 1853 Friedrich Wieck published a treatise dedicated to both subjects, *Clavier und Gesang*. He compared these two practices, these two techniques, to connect them to a common aesthetic base. Weick's treatise is the main source upon which I will base my argument.

In chapters 9 and 10, Wieck gave a very precise description of the Italian vocal technique he taught. We easily recognise the bel canto tradition from eighteenth-century accounts.[6] The basic principles of that school are a naturally beautiful voice, a supple and easy vocal emission, regulation of the breath, evenness of tone from the low to the high range, and blended registers.

The vocal practice summarised by Wieck was the very one cherished by Chopin. That they admired the same performers is significant. For instance, the singer Wieck praised the most in his book was Jenny Lind, known as the "Swedish Nightingale" because her pure technique and supple voice gave an impression of great ease. Wieck (1988, 81) particularly praised the extraordinary nuance she applied to *piano* and *pianissimo* singing. This might seem to be a passing comment made by him, easily overlooked, but it matches precisely Chopin's observations when he heard that singer in London in 1848, singing Bellini's *La Sonnambula* and conducted by Mendelssohn: "She impresses me as a remarkable Swedish type, surrounded not by an ordinary halo but by a kind of Northern Lights. She produces an extraordinary effect in

6. For a definition of bel canto technique and its chronology see Toft (2013, 1–20).

La Sonnambula. She sings with amazing purity and certainty, and her *piano* is so steady—as smooth and even as a thread of hair" (Chopin 1962, 315).[7]

Wieck, like Chopin, admired *La Sonnambula*, in which he believed the writing was truly vocal. Adelina Patti's recordings are very precious because she studied with musicians who had been involved in the first performances of some of Bellini's operas. Consequently, we can take her style as historically authentic. She was sixty-three when she recorded the aria "Ah! non credea mirarti" from *La Sonnambula*, and we must remember that this is a very early recording, made in 1906. Nevertheless, it is obvious that there is a great distance between this bel canto and our current preference for powerful voices that project the sound (Patti 1906). At least five other very interesting qualities can be observed:

1. a very light vibrato overall;
2. the use, however, of some special effects on certain notes for expressive purposes—in particular, a kind of vocal tremolo which is very different from our modern conception of the vibrato;
3. a linear rubato that is characteristic of bel canto and comes from the *sprezzatura* of the *seconda pratica*, and in which the singer is completely independent of the orchestra, which plays strictly in time;[8]
4. flexibility of tempo, including the use of accelerando and ritardando;
5. the use of extemporised embellishments in specific places, a tradition that had been passed on from the first performance.[9]

7. From a letter to Albert Grzymama dated 11 May 1848. "C'est une Suédoise hors de pair. Ce ne sont pas des lueurs habituelles qui l'illuminent, mais une sorte d'aurore boréale. Elle fait énnormément d'effet dans la *Somnambule*. Elle chante avec assurance et pureté; son piano est aussi égal et continu qu'un cheveu" (Chopin 1953–60, 3:342 [letter 717]).

8. See Rowland (1994) and, for an overview of the question, Hudson (1994).

9. See Eigeldinger's comments (Eigeldinger and Goy 2006, 114).

The singing tone

The connection between vocal and pianistic techniques as taught by Wieck is obvious. In chapter 8, he writes explicitly that pianists must practise touch as singers practise tone. The same relaxation and ease are required, and beauty of sound is ensured by a perfectly controlled technique: "a good and fluent tone produced with limber and relaxed fingers and cooperative and flexible wrists without assistance from the arms" (Wieck 1988, 64).

The voice shouldn't be overworked; and the same applies to the piano, which shouldn't be played beyond its limits. In this, Wieck's teaching is closely parallel to Chopin's, as the latter insisted on the importance of sound quality and ease of playing. His students reported that he always wanted them to play in a flowing way. For Chopin as for Jenny Lind, an easy production of tone wasn't compatible with the sound projection required in very large rooms. Chopin preferred playing in salons, and the greater part of Lind's career was as a recitalist and oratorio singer. Numerous accounts indicate that Chopin's tone palette included nuances that are hardly audible. I will give several examples.

In chapter 12, Wieck insists that fingers must "play into the keys with a certain firmness, decisiveness, speed and strength" (Wieck 1988, 102). Without this, it is impossible to perform a portamento, a staccato, or an accent on the piano. He draws attention to the use of various types of touch on a very small scale. Chopin similarly advocated variety in touch, and this explains his insistence on individuality of the fingers, a matter to be developed rather than resisted: "As many sounds as there are fingers—everything is a matter of knowing . . . good fingering" (Chopin 1993, 74, 76, as translated in Eigeldinger 1986, 195).

His fingerings are evidently associated with vocal practices. According to Manuel García, different tones colour different vocal ranges. There are two principal timbres: light and dark (García 1847, part 1:6).[10] García described precisely how the

10. ". . . deux timbres principaux: le timbre clair; et le timbre sombre." An alternative translation is "clear" and "sombre" (see García [1972] 1984, xli).

larynx moves to enable a singer to produce such tones (ibid., part 1:15). At the end of his treatise, García explained in detail the performance of an aria by Rossini (see figure 1). We notice that the singer is instructed to alternate between the various tone qualities to give an expressive performance of the melody.[11] This way of colouring the melodic line according to the text has completely disappeared today.

Figure 1. Manuel García, *Traité complet de l'Art du Chant* (1847, part 2:104): Rossini, *Semiramide*, Scena e Aria

11. See the summary in Toft (2013, 86–88), which underlines the importance of Manuel García's contribution.

I think these vocal colours can be adapted to the piano. In Chopin's works, specific fingerings could correspond to these qualities. The first of the three études published in the *Méthode des méthodes* begins with a representation of a female chest voice, coloured by the dark tone described earlier, which, García says, "makes the chest voice round, full and sweet" (García 1847 part 1:23, as translated in García [1972] 1984, 31).[12] In bars 42–43 and again in bars 46–47, the thumb is used on three consecutive notes (see figure 2). The heaviness and slowness of that finger could suggest the guttural tone that is also described by García (1847 part 1:15).[13] The opposite effect is evident in a very soft passage in the E♭-major nocturne, op. 9, no. 2 (figure 3): the use of the fifth finger on consecutive notes (bar 26) could produce a light tone that resembles a head voice. This would correspond to the image of very pure and clear tone described by García and practiced by Jenny Lind.[14]

These tones have nothing to do with the colour that corresponds to a specific range, with respect to either voice or piano. The tones are produced by the way the finger strikes and the speed with which it moves. However, it is obvious that Chopin also made the most of the very specific colours of the ranges on a Viennese piano or a Pleyel. This sensitivity to a register's particular colour also comes from vocal models. Maria Malibran and Giuditta Pasta were famed for producing feminine tones in the high register and masculine ones in the low register. This androgynous quality in female voices was highly appreciated.

12. ". . . la voix de poitrine ronde, pleine et douce."
13. For an English translation, see García ([1972] 1984, lxi).
14. This way of singing, characteristic of the art of Jenny Lind, is raised notably both by Chopin, in the letter quoted above, and by Wieck, in several places in which his text specifically extols the singer. The latter can be usefully consulted by means of the index to the English translation (Wieck 1988).

Figure 2. Frédéric Chopin, Etude in F Minor, from the *Méthode des méthodes*, bars 42–50. Use of the thumb on consecutive notes

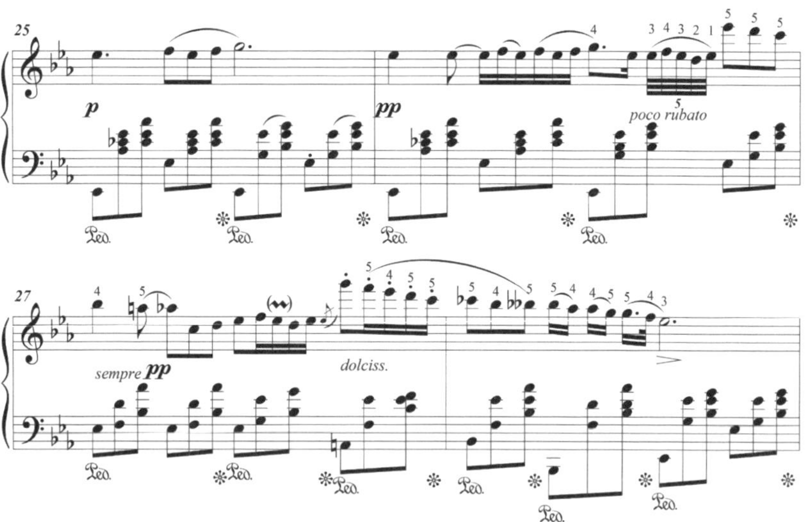

Figure 3. Frédéric Chopin, Nocturne in E♭ Major, op. 9, no. 2, bars 25–28. Use of the fifth finger on consecutive notes

Ornamentation: the "Golden Rule"

Ornamentation on the piano has much in common with bel canto and with the rhetorical conception, inherited from the eighteenth century, that music is a kind of speech. In an interview near the end of her life, the English pianist Adelina de Lara (1872–1961), a student of Clara Schumann, gave a valuable example. In performing Chopin's portrait from Robert Schumann's *Carnaval*, de Lara played it exactly the way she heard it played by Madam Schumann, respecting the "Golden Rule" her teacher taught her: the same thing must never be said twice in the same way. In this way she continued the imitation implicit in the music: by performing the repeat *mezza voce* and with a notable use of rubato, Adelina de Lara somehow imitated Chopin's playing by performing Robert's imitation as Clara did (De Lara 1996, track 2).

Linear rubato

Rubato was an important expressive device for Chopin and Clara Schumann. They both used a linear rubato that was borrowed from the Italian singers who had continued to apply *sprezzatura* and perform in the tradition of *seconda pratica*. By listening to pianists trained in Chopin's tradition and to pianists directly trained by Clara Schumann, we may grasp this performing style.[15] Fanny Davies (1861–1934) was another English student of Clara, and she recorded several works by Robert Schumann in the late 1920s. In her playing we easily recognise this type of linear rubato, in which notes are arpeggiated not only between the hands but also between the voices, so that the melodic lines can be heard distinctly.[16] Because of this very linear approach to piano textures, left and right hands are constantly heard playing one after the

15. For example, listen to Raoul Koczalski, a student of Karol Mikuli, performing the Nocturne op. 27 no. 2 (1928) or the Nocturne op. 9 no. 1 (ca. 1938) (Eigeldinger 2006, CD tracks 12 and 13).

16. Listen to Fanny Davies's 1929 performance of no. 10 from the *Kinderscenen* on De Lara, Eibenschütz, and Davies (1991, CD 1, track 2).

other. Such playing is characteristic of performances by pianists from Chopin's tradition and especially by Clara's students.[17]

Articulation and phrasing: a matter of breathing

Wieck, as well as Chopin, placed importance on the use of the wrist as an essential aspect of technique. This too is connected to the Viennese fortepiano school and the Italian vocal tradition from the eighteenth century; by means of the wrist, a pianist can place articulations in the musical phrase. In that respect, the wrist is to a pianist what the breath is to a singer. In his sketch for a piano method, Chopin wrote, "the wrist: respiration in the voice" (Chopin 1993, 76, as translated in Eigeldinger 1986, 45). And in his teaching he is known to have insisted particularly on this specific role of the wrist. Where and how should one breathe? A pianist must ask that question, just as a singer does.

Clara Schumann didn't publish a piano method, but Adelina de Lara explained how important written articulations were for her. Madam Schumann played, she said, to make what she wished her students to do very easy to grasp. "She insisted on perfect phrasing of quick passages such as those in the last movement of the A minor concerto" (De Lara 1996, track 2, 2:29). De Lara then performed the section beginning in bar 144 the way she heard it played by her teacher. Although this example isn't explicitly concerned with the voice, it shows clearly how articulations could be read without breaking away abruptly from eighteenth-century traditions. This way of performing slurs, inherited from the past, also has implications for accentuation and rhythm. Adelina described "a balance without any undue accent, a sort of swaying movement, hardly perceptible, but it is there," illustrating her remarks with the opening of the third movement of the Fantasy, op. 17, and the first movement of the Concerto, op. 54, beginning with bar 67.

As a singer uses breathing to articulate the melodic lines which shape the phrases, so must the pianist also organise his or

17. Listen to Fanny Davies's 1929 performance of no. 1 from the *Kinderscenen* (ibid.).

her instrument's "speech." We often encounter slurs that must be interpreted according to the context. The de Lara interview and recordings indicate that, for Clara Schumann's students, slurs never indicated a simple legato. As in the eighteenth-century, a series of slurs meant that the articulation of short figures had to be emphasised more or less, according to the character of the piece. Unfortunately, scores are no longer seen in that light, even though we tend to use only urtext editions.

Synthesis

Clara's own works shouldn't be neglected as sources of information, especially the *Soirées musicales*, op.6, composed between 1834 and 1836 (published in Leipzig and Paris in 1836). She was then sixteen years old. This was a masterstroke Liszt didn't fail to notice: he played the *Soirées* in Vienna in April 1838. Together with her previous opus (no. 5), these pieces form a group of ten pieces that are characteristic, poetic, and inspired by Chopin, Schumann, and Mendelssohn. Schumann also noticed how valuable this work was: in 1837 he published a review of it in which he ranked her among the best composers of characteristic pieces (Schumann 1837). The Nocturne (figure 4) is a tribute to Chopin, new master of this art, and it reveals a perfect knowledge of the singing school as her father had taught her. The score is conceived so as to guide the right hand. The notation gives the impression that we are attending a singing lesson.

Andante con moto
sempre legato
dolce
Ped.
6
sf
11
rf
rubato stretto
cresc.
16
sf
pp
ritenuto e legato.
pf il canto marcato

20
e poco a poco morendo.
pp
25
tr
p
30
11
risoluto
cresc.
f
p
34
rinforz.
8
mf
Ped.

Figure 4. Clara Schumann, Nocturne, from *Soirées musicales*, op. 6, bars 1–58

Here are some examples from the Nocturne (figure 4):

Bars 7–8: We can notice the variety and precision of touch that are required.

Bar 11: The small note indicates a portamento. This way of singing a new syllable by approaching it from the previous note (the lower in Clara's Nocturne) was criticised by García[18] but described elsewhere, for example by Vaccai in his *Metodo pratico di canto italiano* (1832, lesson 13), as a second type of portamento.

Bar 15: A linear rubato is expressed by syncopations. *Rubato stretto* indicates a slight acceleration caused by emotion. *Stretto* is an indication Chopin often used in his youthful works. The added accents could suggest the use of vibrato as an expressive ornament. Bellini and Donizetti wrote such accents on the light syllables of some words or at the end of sentences, and these surely must be understood as indicating vibrato rather than a dynamic accent. The notation corresponds exactly to the example given by García in figure 5.

(1) Quelques auteurs appellent cela faire vibrer la voix (*vibrar la voce*). M. Catruffo, dans sa méthode de vocalisation, indique cet effet au moyen des syncopes.

Figure 5. Manuel García, *Traité complet de l'Art du Chant* (1847 part 1:61). Notational use of accents to indicate vibrato

Bars 17–18: The key is struck with different speeds to produce the *sf* followed by *pp*; this can suggest use of different vocal tones in the same range. The rest indicates a *mezzo respire*, to which I will return below.

18. "The portamento is performed by leading the syllable which one is going to leave, and not, as it is too often done in France, with the following syllable taken by anticipation" (García 1972 [1975], 84). ("Le port de voix s'exécute en conduisant la voix avec la syllable que l'on va abandonner, et non pas, comme on le fait trop souvent en France, avec la syllable suivante prise par anticipation" [García 1847, part 2:28].)

Bar 19: The indication "*pf il canto marcato*" probably parallels the use of a round or dark tone in the low register of a female voice.

Bar 30: Clara added here a very old ornament that derives from Caccini's *trillo*. García complained that it had gradually fallen out of use (see figure 6). He suggested that the maximum speed should be four repetitions of the note as semiquavers, at crochet equals 100 on Maelzel's metronome. This ornament creates a variation in intensity; it differs from the vibrato, which creates a variation in pitch.

(1) Aujourd'hui aucun chanteur, excepté Mme Damoreau, ne serait préparé à l'exécution du trait suivant, quoique bien simple :

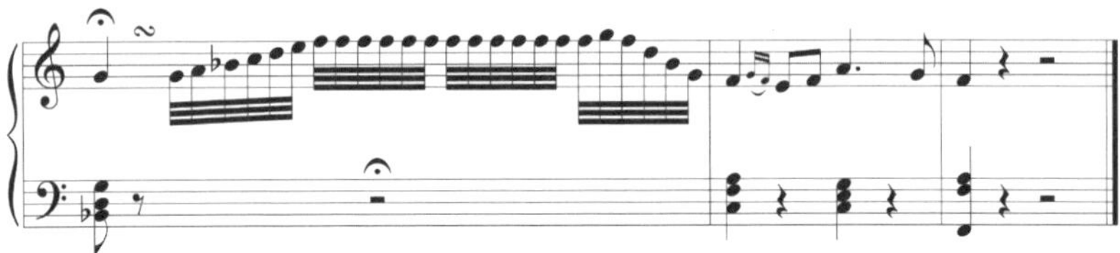

Figure 6. Manuel García, *Traité complet de l'Art du Chant* (1847, part 1:61). Notation of *trillo* ("sons martelés")

Bar 36: This figuration requires that the thumb be used several times in succession. It also includes an indication of tonal contrast.

Bars 50 and 54: Again rubato is notated, this time together with very specific indications of sound colour. To enhance the structural articulation of the nocturne, the composer clearly suggests using *martellato* (dots under a slur) at this point to colour the melody. This mode of emitting sound is described by García as a pulse of air on each note, produced by pressure from the stomach and dilation of the pharynx (García 1847, part 1:30; [1972] 1984, 219). This way of initiating sounds by pressing on each individual note would be combined by the skilful performer with a subtle use of vibrato as suggested by accents on certain notes.

But the essential problem is to rebuild vocal images that can be identified and applied today. In Schumann's time, these images were precise, since they were linked to living singers. Chopin's students recalled that Rubini or Malibran were taken as models (Eigeldinger 1986, 45). In a lesson described by Wieck (1988,

132), he played for his student a theme from *Il pirata* by Bellini as he had heard it sung by Rubini. Present-day reconstruction efforts rely upon other instances, with naturally different results, but they are useful in opening up new horizons for the performers' imaginations.

MUSICIANS OF THE FUTURE: THE ENERGY IN SPEECH

The beautiful Italian singing that Wieck and Chopin both transferred to the piano was opposed by a new school that was just being established. In his treatise, Friedrich Wieck vigorously objected to new vocal models required by Berlioz in his *Benvenuto Cellini* and especially by Wagner. Wagner, he writes, is a "creative genius," but his music is not "singable"; and Berlioz chokes the voices under a heavy orchestra (Wieck 1988, 49, 117–18). The new, modern school was turned towards another direction, looking for the sublime in the energy of speech. Wieck particularly attacked the Parisian singers and pianists associated with it.

In France, Gilbert Duprez represented that school. He had sung in the first performance of *Cellini* in 1838, after his talent as *tenore di forza* had been discovered the year before in *Guillaume Tell*. He is said to have been the first tenor to sing the top C as a chest tone in *Guillaume Tell*, much to the dismay of Rossini. Indeed, the search for the energy of speech had many musical consequences: the chest voice was extended; the vibrato was extended; performances were created which were sometimes considered to be overdone, in which acting was more important than singing. In the music intended for this new technique, a declamatory and syllabic writing was favoured, in the style of the recitative. García's description of this style was in agreement with Wieck's, though less polemical:

> Declamatory songs are nearly always monosyllabic; they exclude almost all vocalization. This style, created for the impassioned feelings, undoubtedly has recourse to the musical accents, but its principal effect rests upon the dramatic accent. The singer should, as a consequence, make everything converge to this end. The syllabication, the grammatical quality, the very well graduated strength of the voice,

> the timbres, the bold accents, the sighs, the expressive and unexpected transitions, and finally some appoggiaturas and portamentos, such are the elements to which he has recourse.
>
> The diction should be not only correct, but noble, lofty; the affected, trivial and exaggerated forms are suitable only in parody and in comic caricatures [*buffi caricati*]. In order to excel in the dramatic style, it is necessary to have a soul of fire, a gigantic power; the actor should constantly dominate the singer.[19] But one should be careful to approach this style only with moderation and reserve, for it quickly exhausts the resources of the voice. Only the singer whose constitution is strong, but who, through a long practice of his art, has lost the freshness, the youth and the flexibility of the voice, should adopt it. The use of it is reserved for the final period of his talent. (García 1847, part 2:70, as translated in García [1972] 1975 200–201)[20]

Wieck condemned this technique because it ruined the voice; its effects, he argued, were proved by Duprez himself, a victim of the vocally disastrous practice, now widespread, that he had set at the head of his teaching. In Duprez's method, the "large, expressive and powerful style" is taught first (Duprez 1846, title page, my translation).[21] It predominates throughout; in fact, it is the only topic of the first part. This contrasts significantly with García's method, which contains only a couple of paragraphs on that

19. Mr. Duprez, Madame Schroeder Devrient. [García's footnote]

20. "Les chants dramatiques sont presque toujours monosyllabiques ; ils excluent à peu près toute vocalisation. Ce genre, fait pour les sentiments passionnés, a sans doute recours aux accents musicaux, mais son effet principal repose sur l'accent dramatique. Le chanteur doit, par conséquent, faire tout converger vers ce but. La syllabation, la quantité grammaticale, la force de la voix bien graduée, les timbres, les accents hardis, les soupirs, les transitions expressives et inattendues, enfin quelques appoggiatures et ports de voix, tels sont les éléments auxquels il a recours.

La diction doit être non seulement juste, mais noble, élevée ; les formes affectées, triviales, exagérées, ne conviennent u'à la parodie, aux *buffi caricati*. Pour exceller dans le style dramatique, il faut une âme de feu, une puissance gigantesque : l'acteur doit constamment dominer le chanteur (M. Duprez, Madame Schroeder-Devrient). Mais on aura soin de l'aborder ce genre qu'avec modération et réserve car il épuise promptement les ressources de la voix. Le chanteur dont la constitution est consolidée, mais qui, par un long exercice de son art, a perdu la fraîcheur, la jeunesse et la flexibilité de la voix, doit seul l'aborder. L'emploi en est réservé à la deuxième période de son talent."

21. "Style large d'expression et de force."

topic (see above). For Duprez, power in the voice is to be sought before qualities such as suppleness and agility. We also notice that the technical advice given by Duprez is extremely simplified. Duprez's teaching, as represented in his method, would seem to represent a considerable decline when compared with García's. But caution is needed before drawing such conclusions. What is clear at the beginning of the first chapter is that the French singer was radically opposed to the scientific approach of the Italian singer: "It would be out of place and perhaps distressing in such a treatise to give a scientific and physical definition of the larynx, the trachea, the lungs and so on ... As a poet doesn't need to know the physiology of the brain to write verses, a singer doesn't need to know the anatomy of the vocal organs to sing" (Duprez 1846, 2, my translation).[22]

It is interesting to observe the notation that is used for this vocal style (see figure 7). Duprez placed *marcato* symbols above the notes to indicate the projection of the voice, with vibrato, and above the example he wrote: "Martial. Forceful style and vibrated. This piece must be sung with full voice overall, and in some passages the voice should be softened affectionately" (ibid., 56, my translation). It should be noted that the effect of the forceful, vibrated style is enhanced by the presence of very contrasted soft and legato passages.

The same technique is explained clearly by Alexis de Garaudé, who taught singing at the Paris Conservatoire from 1816 until 1841 and wrote an important method that was republished several times between 1809 and 1854. He reports the use of two alternative notations (see figure 8) and provides additional comments:

22. "Il serait déplacé et peut-ètre affligeant dans un traité de cette nature de donner une definition scientifique et physique du larynx, de la trache, des poumons, & & & . . . De meme qu'un poète n'a pas besoin de connaître physiologie du cerveau pour faire des vers, de meme il est inutile de savoir l'anatomie des organes vocaux pour chanter."

Martial. **Style de force et vibré. Il faut chanter ce morceau sur le plein de la voix en général, et dans quelques passages, adoucir affectueusement.**

Figure 7. Gilbert-Louis Duprez, *L'art du chant* (1846, 56). Notation of the "forceful" style

There are two ways of producing this effect:

1. by a very short sustained sound which is usually indicated by an arrow-like symbol placed above the note; for example . . .
2. (2nd) by the following inflection [example with accents]. . . .

This way of attacking the sound with strength bears a resemblance to the effect that a singer tries to produce with his voice when he wants to get an echo in a vault. In Italian music, one often uses this vibration, the effect of which is to give the voice all the sonority of which it is capable and to mark the musical phrase. However, one must not misuse it, as some singers do. In singing, it must be mainly used on the accented syllables of each word, on appoggiaturas or grace notes, and on strong beats of the bar, where the character requires a more pronounced colour. (Garaudé [1841?], 39, my translation)

De la VIBRATION DE LA VOIX

Cet effet peut se produire de deux manières:
1. par un son filé très court, qui s'indique ordinairement par une enflèchure posée sur la Note; exemple

2. par l'inflexion suivante

Cette manière d'attaquer le son avec force a quelque ressemblance avec l'effet qu'on cherche à produire avec sa voix lorsqu'on veut faire résonner l'écho d'une voûte. Dans la musique Italienne, on emploie fréquemment cette vibration, dont l'effet est de donner à la voix toute la sonorité dont elle est susceptible, et d'accentuer la phrase musicale. Il ne faut cependant pas en abuser, comme font quelques chanteurs. Dans le chant, on doit principalement en faire usage sur les Syllabes où est situé l'accent de chaque mot, sur les appogiatures ou petites Notes, et sur les tems forts de la mesure, dont le caractère demande un coloris plus prononcé.

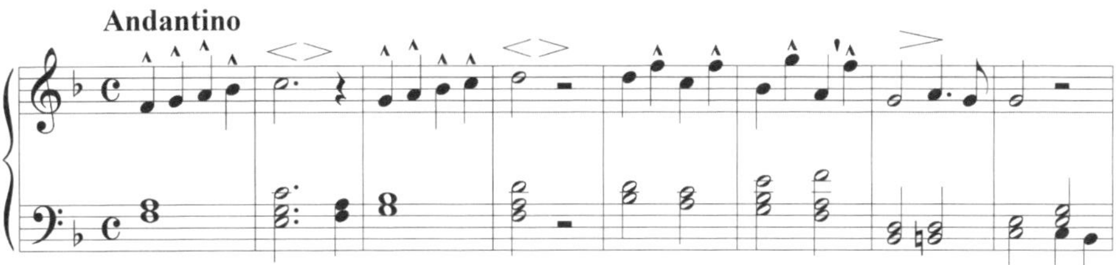

Figure 8. Alexis de Garaudé, *Méthode complète de chant* ([1841?], 39). Alternative notations for strong attacks

It should be noted that García also describes another technique, which he indicates by a wavy line (see figure 9): the tremolo, which is a trembling or quivering of the voice justified by the dramatic situation. All these descriptions, taken together, show that vibrato was associated with more varied effects than nowadays, as was demonstrated in Adelina Patti's recording.[23] Although Garaudé warned against misusing vibrato his choice of standard symbols, which were easy to engrave, indicates that by mid-century this vocal colouring was increasingly used in a more uniform manner.

Figure 9. Manuel García, *Traité complet de l'Art du Chant* (1847, part 2:53). Notation for tremolo

In the singing of Hermann Winkelmann, the oldest Wagnerian tenor to make recordings, we can hear the heroic and declamatory sound of the new singing school. Winkelmann never recorded any Wagner, but his voice can be heard in an aria from *Dalibor* by Smetana, recorded in 1905 (Burton 2002, CD track 19). The writing here is more syllabic than in Italian music and therefore more favourable for sound projection in the new style.

The new style represented by Duprez embraced a rhetoric of excess, and this was also displayed by pianists. Declamatory power

23. See the summary by Robert Toft (2013, 92–99), which attempts to distinguish four types of vibrato in the various sources.

and the energy of speech characterise the pianists whose performance style contrasted most strongly with the style of Chopin and Clara Schumann. And the virtuoso whom Wieck singled out (but did not name) for mistreating pianos was, of course, Liszt (Wieck 1988; see chapters 6 and 7 and my comments below). The opposition between the two schools isn't merely a product of historical musicology; it was noted at the time. We see it in a famous caricature of Pauline Viardot, who studied with both Liszt and Chopin (figure 10). She is at the piano with Chopin, who says to her, "That's the 'Liszt' way of playing! You mustn't play like that when accompanying the voice" (as translated in Eigeldinger 1986, 187).[24]

Figure 10. Chopin and Pauline Viardot; ink drawing by Maurice Sand, 1844. Reproduced from Eigeldinger (1986, 187)

24. "Ça c'est le jeu de 'Liszt'! Il n'en faut pas pour accompagner la voix."

Chopin versus Liszt

The *Hexaméron*, a collective work,[25] provides a very useful comparison of these two conceptions of pianistic style, which coexisted until the twentieth century. The six pianist-composers each treated the theme, taken from Bellini's opera *I Puritani*, in a very characteristic way. I propose to compare the variations composed by Liszt and Chopin.

Chopin unfolds a large cantilena, *sotto voce* (see figure 11). The accompaniment is regular, its texture is homogeneous. Phrase marks are placed according to the principles of the Italian school of singing: *respiro* and *mezzo-respiro* (full and half breaths) should correspond as much as possible to the phrase division. Long phrases require conservation of breath, especially in a cantabile passage, and this prevents the singer from pushing the sound.

25. By Liszt, Thalberg, Pixis, Herz, Czerny, and Chopin (1839).

Largo
sotto voce
ff

radolcendo
pp
CHOPIN
ppp
les 2 Ped.
trem.

Figure 11. Hexaméron, Variation 6 by Chopin, with coda by Liszt

In order to sing with more power, one must use more breath and thus breathe more often. Independently of the musical style, the vocal sound sought by the new school resulted in a new way of phrasing. This can be noticed in Duprez's method (see figure 12). In a very simple exercise, the first breath is placed very early, implying that the singer is required to use a large amount of breath.

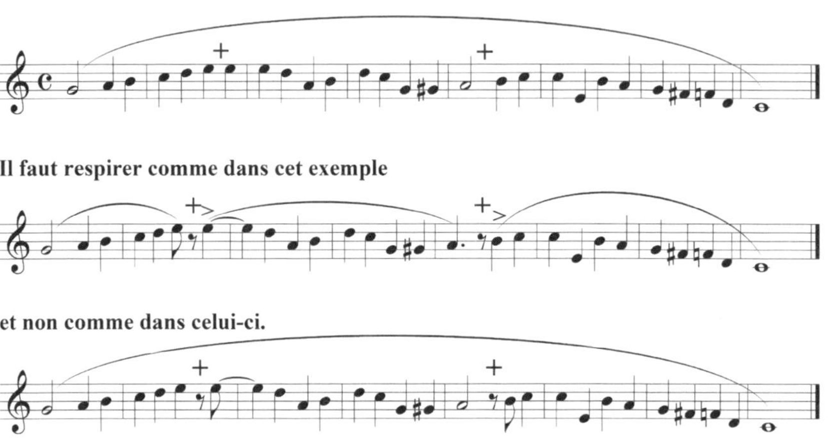

Figure 12. Duprez, *L'art du chant* (1846, 6)

Liszt's variation is based on an approach to phrasing that is quite different from Chopin's and that corresponds to this new school (see figure 13). This variation is preceded by an "orchestral" introduction (bars 1–16); Liszt, like Berlioz and Wagner, thought of the orchestra as a dramatic character. Even when the singing starts, the orchestra doesn't recede; it remains present, playing a counterpoint with which the singer must compete. Therefore the singing itself is more projected: Liszt plays "en relief," a description that can be traced back to Wilhelm von Lenz (see Lenz 1983; 1995, 77).

Moderato
sempre marcato il tema
mf
nobilmente
sf
mp
poco rit.
dol. armonioso
precipitato
f
marcato
sf

poco ritenuto
15
8va
sotto voce
p
dolente
(8va)
18
8va
21
cresc.
f appassionato
(8va)
24
loco
stringendo

Figure 13. Hexaméron, Variation 2 by Liszt

With this aim in view, the melody is divided in short fragments, as would follow if a great amount of breath were being spent. It is immediately coloured with staccato and slurs. Such inflections were reserved for very specific affects—specifically, to express pain—in the old Italian school; they become commonplace in Liszt's scores. It is because of this that Wieck and Chopin blamed him for affectation and excess. On the second page (bars 27–28), we see again the accents indicating a vibrato. The pedal is depressed in longer units than in Chopin's music, to enable the piano to resonate more and be more powerful. The differences in the resulting sound are consistent with the different pianos these two virtuosos preferred. A Pleyel piano, Chopin's favourite, has very precise dampers, after the Viennese manner; this means that the sound is perfectly damped. The Erard pianos favoured by Liszt allow one to play with more resonance and density of sound, a kind of *sfumato* that is typical of English pianos. As a result, Liszt tends towards more powerful dynamics, from *p* to *fff* (Chopin's dynamic range is from *pp* to *ff*). Moreover, even in the introduction we can see some agogic indications that require the "orchestra" to play in a flexible tempo. From this, it may be deduced that Liszt's singing rubato is different from Chopin's, which corresponds to eighteenth-century bel canto: Liszt's is a more vertical rubato, closer to present-day practice.

We must return to Chopin's variation to consider the coda Liszt composed. Liszt undoubtedly wanted to pay a tribute to Chopin by imitating his performance style. The music is his own in some respects—chords, progressions, tremolos—but as if played by Chopin. The dynamics are extreme but focused on nuances of *piano*; a *pppp* occurs near the end, followed by the indication *estinto*. We see the extent to which the sound quality of "almost nothing" is associated with Chopin. We might also notice the indication in bar 18 to use both pedals. Chopin indicated the una corda only once (in the Nocturne op.15 no. 2), but there is strong evidence that he subtly used both pedals to produce special effects.

A strong advocate of bel canto aesthetics at the piano

Wieck's chapters 6 and 7 concern pedalling, and in them Wieck expressed in the clearest way possible his opposition to the Parisian pianists, making particular allusion to Liszt.[26] One sentence is unequivocal: "The ladies dissolve in rapture over the long-haired, pale, apostle of art" (Wieck 1988, 57). Wieck clearly believed that vocal music should be the guide: "The nearer the piano comes to the singing voice, the better" (54). But, as noted earlier, such statements don't say precisely which vocal (and therefore pianistic) style is to be followed. It is only by reading the criticism that is explicitly expressed in these two chapters that we can finally understand which performance style he strongly rejected: the constant use of the pedals, a vehement (thundering, bravura) style, and violent contrasts:

> Two big bravura pieces were thundered out with the sustaining pedal down. They were sometimes suddenly whispered, too, the continued reverberation of the thirteen quaking, deepest bass notes, left over from the fortissimo, providing the essential foundation. . . . Do these piano pounders really think it beautiful to depress the pedal for every measure? (53)

This playing style suppresses all the rests and the punctuation of the speech. The sound, made constant by overuse of the pedal, lacks significance:

> Piano playing, to be sure, but what kind of piano playing? Mostly nothing but a continuous jumble of the most diverse chords, without cadences, without points of rest—ludicrous passages covered by the sustaining pedal, unintelligible thunder in the bass with the pedal down, or again, by way of a change, a meagre, stiff, thin touch supported by the pedal. (55)

Wieck criticised a type of virtuosity that is artistically worthless, a rhetoric of excess expressed by effects of colour and theatricality:

26. See David Rowland's *A History of Pianoforte Pedalling* (1993), which traces the technical history of this opposition between two aesthetics of sound.

> It's a big i.e., long, difficult etude with the most intricate passages, an original confection, perhaps, with some such titles as "In the Depths of the Ocean," or "In Hades," or "What Occurs to Me in a Fit of Madness," hammered out with ghastly exhibitionism and with the pedal applied to the most astonishing harmonies. (55)
>
> . . . and suddenly experience feeling! There is *piano* or *pianissimo*, and no longer content with one pedal, they now shift right in the middle of all the pedal chaos. O, what languishing, what murmuring, what bell-like tones—what a feeling for the soft pedal, what tender sentiment! God! The ladies dissolve in rapture over the long-haired, pale, apostle of art. (57)

Wieck's protest is not merely technical; it is the expression of a major aesthetic issue. In the first excerpt above, Wieck imagined the possible title of the étude. In the second excerpt, he compared the effect produced by the una corda pedal with the sound of a bell. Such references to the external world were characteristic of programme music, and Wieck thereby alluded to musicians he had named in other chapters: Berlioz and Wagner for the voice and Liszt for the piano. These chapters confirm that the real topic of Wieck's treatise is aesthetics, at the time when Hanslick was just publishing his book *Vom Musikalisch-Schönen*. In Chapter 16, it is clear that Wieck considered the style he defended to be old-fashioned. This is why he defined himself in the first pages as "Der alte Schulmeister." But he challenged the progressive artistic vision of his opponents, adopting a truly German attitude: like Goethe, he put forward an eternal classicism against romantic excesses.[27] To those who said, "higher beauty, burial of the past, immersion in the work of art, genius be free" (Wieck 1988, 180), he retorted, "There are unreceptive times, but what is eternal will find its time" (179).

27. This conception of Classicism and Romanticism not as sequential historical periods but as poles in dialectical tension—that is, as aesthetic positions and universal categories existing concurrently—is one of the most interesting aspects of Goethe's views about art. Wieck's position reflects the authority that this concept carried throughout the nineteenth century everywhere that Germanic culture prevailed.

This classicism was defended by others: Mendelssohn in Leipzig, Moscheles in London, Chopin and Heller in Paris, Schumann in Düsseldorf. By the end of the century, the German conservatories had become places of worship dedicated to eternal classicism, and Clara Schumann supervised the piano teaching in Frankfurt.[28] Liszt, who always hated the conservatories and especially the one in Paris, made fun of the German schools. In one of his master classes in 1884, Liszt criticised a student who was playing a nocturne by Chopin:

> The first lady played the theme at the beginning extremely sentimentally and fragmented, whereupon the master sat down and played the theme in an extremely broad and expansive manner. The young lady continually swayed along back and forth, to which Liszt said, "Keep perfectly calm, child. This tottering is 'frankfurtisch,' just do not totter so." He sat down and said: "Even the wonderful [Clara] Schumann sways like that," and he humorously imitated it. Then he came to speak about the fashionable fragmenting of all the themes and said: "Disgusting! I thank you, that is certainly the opposite of good manners." Then in an extremely droll manner he imitated Moscheles playing one of his etudes. . . . Then he said: "Yes, in Leipzig, or Frankfurt or Cologne or Berlin at the 'great conservatories,' there you will make a success with that." "One can say to you as to Ophelia: 'get thee to a nunnery,' get thee to a conservatory." (Zimdars 1996, 22)[29]

To another student, who played his first *Liebestraum*, he said: "You must play that totally carried away as if you were not even seated at the piano, completely lost to the world; not 1, 2, 3, 4 as in the Leipzig Conservatory!" (ibid., 47; Hamilton 2008, 191).

---

28. Studies of violinists at the end of the nineteenth century have produced similar conclusions. See David Milsom's recent article "The Franco-Belgian School of Violin Playing" (2013), following his 2003 book, which underlines the rhetorical opposition between a German "classical" school, represented by Joachim, and a Franco-Belgian school that seeks to be different.
29. See also Hamilton (2008, 191).

SUMMARY

To conclude, I would like to emphasise that two types of vocality are at the core of the conflict that set Chopin and Clara Schumann in opposition to Liszt. In my opinion, three points are essential:

First, their different conceptions of a desirable sound:

a. Always beautiful for Clara and Chopin, it must be sublime for Liszt. These different aesthetic positions have considerable consequences for technique for both singers and pianists.
b. Sound should be emitted naturally, rather than projected "in relief."
c. Singers should save breath, rather than spending it for the sake of power.
d. Pianists should apply technique, especially when pedalling, that serves clarity and transparency rather than resonance.

Second, their different phrasing:

a. Bel canto, as opposed to the new, "Wagnerian" style of singing;
b. Based on rhetoric and speech, rather than a purely musical energy.

Third, their different conception of music:

a. Respect for the legacy of the past, as opposed to breaking with it for the sake of modernity;
b. Belief in "absolute music," rather than "music of the future."

These oppositions reveal a paradox. "Absolute music," allegedly conceived without any reference to the world, keeps alive a practice that is based on speech. "Music of the future" is built from innovations that are inspired by the world itself; it advocates liberation from speech in order to create new, specifically musical paths.

REFERENCES

Brown, Clive. 1999. *Classical and Romantic Performing Practice 1750–1900*. Oxford: Oxford University Press.

Burton, Anthony, series ed. 2002. *A Performer's Guide to Music of the Romantic Period*. London: Associated Board of the Royal Schools of Music. Book and compact disc.

Chopin, Frédéric. 1953–60. *Correspondance de Frédéric Chopin*. Translated and edited by Bronislas Édouard Sydow [Bronisław Edward Sydow]. 3 vols. Paris: Richard-Masse. Abridged translation by Arthur Hedley published as Chopin 1962.

———. 1962. *Selected Correspondence of Fryderyk Chopin*. Collected and annotated by Bronisław Edward Sydow. Translated and edited with additional material and a commentary by Arthur Hedley. London: Heinemann. First published as Chopin 1953–60.

———. 1993. *Esquisses pour une méthode de piano*. Edited by Jean-Jacques Eigeldinger. Harmoniques. Paris: Flammarion. Reconstructed from manuscript sources.

Crutchfield, Will. 1990a. "The Classical Era: Voices." In *Performance Practice*, vol. 2: *Music After 1600*, edited by Howard Mayer Brown and Stanley Sadie, 292–319. New York: W. W. Norton.

———. 1990b. "The 19th Century: Voices." In *Performance Practice*, vol. 2: *Music After 1600*, edited by Howard Mayer Brown and Stanley Sadie, 424–58. New York: W. W. Norton.

Czerny, Carl. (1842) 1968. *Erinnerungen aus meinem Leben*. Edited by Walter Kolneder. Sammlung mussikwissenschaftlicher Abhandlungen 46. Strasburg: Éditions P. H. Heitz. Czerny's unpublished manuscript written 1842; first published in full, in a translation by Ernest Sanders, as Czerny 1956.

———. 1956. "Recollections from My Life." Translated by Ernest Sanders. *The Musical Quarterly* 42 (3): 302–17. Translated from the unpublished manuscript *Erinnerungen aus meinem Leben*, written 1842.

De Lara, Adelina. 1996. *Adelina de Lara (1872–1961) Anthology*. Archive Documents, ADCD 2002, compact disc. Recorded 1944–60.

De Lara, Adelina, Ilona Eibenschütz, and Fanny Davies (pianists). 1991. *Pupils of Clara Schumann*. Pearl, GEMM CDS 99049, 6 compact discs. Recorded 1928–52.

Duprez, Gilbert-Louis. 1846. *L'art du chant*. Paris: Au Bureau Central de Musique. Heugel edition (Paris) reproduced in facsimile in *Chant. Les grandes méthodes romantiques de chant; Vol. III: Garcia (père)–Duprez–Rossini*, realised by Jeanne Roudet, Méthodes et Traités. Série II: France 1800–1860 (Courlay, France: Fuzeau, 2005).

Eigeldinger, Jean-Jacques. 1986. *Chopin: Pianist and Teacher as Seen by His Pupils*. Edited by Roy Howat. Translated by Naomi Shohet with Krysia Osostowicz and Roy Howat. Cambridge: Cambridge University Press. First published 1970 as *Chopin vu par ses élèves: Textes recueillis, traduits et commentés* (Neuchâtel: La Baconnière); English edition translated from the 2nd ed. (Neuchâtel: La Baconnière, 1979).

———. 2004. "Chopin et les pianos Pleyel." In *Instruments à claviers—expressivité et flexibilité sonore: Actes des Rencontres internationales Harmoniques, Lausanne, 2002 / Keyboard Instruments—Flexibility of Sound and Expression: Proceedings of the Harmoniques International Congress,* edited by Thomas Steiner, 161–73. Publications de la Société Suisse de Musicologie, 2nd series, 44. Bern: Peter Lang.

———, ed. 2006. *Interpréter Chopin: Actes du colloque des 25 et 26 mai 2005*. Paris: Cité de la musique. Book and compact disc.

———. 2010. *Chopin et Pleyel*. Paris: Fayard.

Eigeldinger, Jean-Jacques, and Pierre Goy. 2006. "Chanter au piano: Enregistrements des années 1903–1938." In Eigeldinger 2006, 110–137.

Fétis, François-Joseph, and Ignaz Moscheles. 1840. *Méthode des Méthodes de Piano, ou traité de l'art de jouer de cet instrument*. Paris: Schlesinger.

Garaudé, Alexis de. [1841?] *Méthode complète de chant; ou, Théorie pratique de cet art*. 2nd ed. Paris: the author. Reproduced in facsimile in *Chant. Les grandes méthodes romantiques de chant; Vol. II: Crescentini–Garaudé*, realised by Jeanne Roudet, Méthodes et Traités. Série II: France 1800–1860 (Courlay, France: Fuzeau, 2005).

García, Manuel Patricio Rodríguez. 1847. *Traité complet de l'art du chant*. 2nd ed. (part 1), 1st ed. (part 2). Paris: the author; E. Troupenas et Cie. Part 1 first published 1840 (Paris: Schott). Reproduced in facsimile in *Chant: Les grandes méthodes romantiques de chant; Vol. 4: Garcia (fils) Cinti-Damoreau–Concone*, realised by Jeanne Roudet, Méthodes et traités. *Série II: France 1800–1860* (Courlay, France:

Fuzeau, 2005). Translated by Donald V. Paschke as García (1972) 1984, (1972) 1975.

———. (1972) 1975. *A Complete Treatise on the Art of Singing: Part Two, Complete and Unabridged.* The editions of 1841 and 1872 collated, edited, and translated by Donald V. Paschke. New York: Da Capo Press. Paschke's translation first published 1972.

———. (1972) 1984. *A Complete Treatise on the Art of Singing [Part 1]: Complete and Unabridged.* The editions of 1841 and 1872 collated, edited, and translated by Donald V. Paschke. New York: Da Capo Press. Paschke's translation first published 1972.

Hamilton, Kenneth. 2008. *After the Golden Age: Romantic Pianism and Modern Performance.* New York: Oxford University Press.

———. 2008b. "Mendelssohn and the Piano." In *Mendelssohn in Performance*, edited by Siegwart Reichwald, 19–40. Bloomington: Indiana University Press.

Hudson, Richard. 1994. *Stolen Time: The History of Tempo Rubato.* Oxford: Oxford University Press / Clarendon Press.

Kroll, Mark. 2007. *Johann Nepomuk Hummel: A Musician's Life and World.* Lanham, MD: Scarecrow Press.

Leech-Wilkinson, Daniel. 2009. *The Changing Sound of Music: Approaches to Studying Recorded Musical Performances.* London: Centre for the History and Analysis of Recorded Music (CHARM). Accessed 28 May 2014. http://www.charm.kcl.ac.uk/studies/chapters/intro.html.

Lenz, Wihelm von. (1971) 1983. *The Great Piano Virtuosos of Our Time: A Classic Account of Studies with Liszt, Chopin, Tausig and Henselt.* Translated by Madeleine R. Baker. Translation revised and edited by Philip Reder. London: Kahn and Averill. This edition first published 1971 (London: Regency Press). Baker's translation first published in English as *The Great Piano Virtuosos of Our Time, from Personal Acquaintance: Liszt, Chopin, Tausig, Henselt* (New York: Schirmer, 1899). Originally published 1872 as *Die großen Pianoforte-Virtuosen unserer Zeit aus persönlicher Bekanntschaft* (Berlin: B. Behr's Buchhandlung [E. Bock]).

———. 1995. *Les grands virtuoses du piano, Liszt, Chopin, Tausig, Henselt.* Translated by Jean-Jacques Eigeldinger. Harmoniques. Paris: Flammarion. Originally published 1872 as *Die großen*

Pianoforte-Virtuosen unserer Zeit aus persönlicher Bekanntschaft (Berlin: B. Behr's Buchhandlung [E. Bock]).

Liszt, Franz, Sigismond Thalberg, Johann Peter Pixis, Henri Herz, Carl Czerny, and Frédéric Chopin. 1839. *Hexaméron: Morceau de concert—Grandes variations de bravoure pour piano sur la Marche des Puritains de Bellini.* Vienna: Haslinger.

Milsom, David. 2003. *Theory and Practice in Late Nineteenth-Century Violin Performance: An Examination of Style in Performance, 1850–1900.* Aldershot, UK: Ashgate.

———. 2013. "The Franco-Belgian School of Violin Playing: Towards an Understanding of Chronology and Characteristics, 1850–1925." *Ad Parnassum: A Journal of Eighteenth- and Nineteenth-Century Instrumental Music* 11 (21): 1–20.

Patti, Adelina (voice). 1906. "Ah! non credea mirarti" by Vincenzo Bellini. Gramophone, 78 rpm, 03084. Copy consulted in the collection of BnF (Bibliothèque nationale de France), département de l'audiovisuel. Also available as track 6 of the compact disc accompanying Eigeldinger 2006.

Peres Da Costa, Neal. 2012. *Off the Record: Performing Practices in Romantic Piano Playing.* New York: Oxford University Press.

Philip, Robert. 1992. *Early Recordings and Musical Style: Changing Tastes in Instrumental Performance, 1900–1950.* Cambridge: Cambridge University Press.

———. 2004. *Performing Music in the Age of Recording.* New Haven, CT: Yale University Press.

Rowland, David. 1993. *A History of Pianoforte Pedalling.* Cambridge: Cambridge University Press.

———. 1994. "Chopin's *tempo rubato* in Context." In *Chopin Studies 2*, edited by John Rink and Jim Samson, 199–213. Cambridge: Cambridge University Press.

Schumann, Robert. 1837. "Soiréen für das Pianoforte von Clara Wieck." *Neue Zeitschrift für Musik* 7 (22): 87.

Steane, John. B. 1974. *The Grand Tradition: Seventy Years of Singing on Record.* London: Duckworth.

Streicher, Johann Andreas. 1801. *Kurze Bemerkungen über das Spielen, Stimmen und Erhalten der Fortepiano.* Wien: mit Albertischen Schriften. Translated as *Brief Remarks on the Playing, Tuning and Maintenance of Fortepianos*, in *The Fortepiano Writings of Streicher,*

Dieudonné, and the Schiedmayers, translated and edited by Preethi de Silva (Lewiston, NY: Edwin Mellen Press, 2008), 38–89.

Toft, Robert. 2013. *Bel Canto: A Performer's Guide*. New York: Oxford University Press.

Vaccai, Nicola. 1832. *Metodo pratico di canto italiano per camera diviso in 15 lezioni, ossiano solfeggi progressivi ed elementari sopra parole di Metastasio*. London: [the author].

Wieck, Friedrich. 1853. *Clavier und Gesang: Didaktisches und Polemisches*. Leipzig: F. Whistling. Translated by Henry Pleasants as Wieck 1988.

———. 1988. *Piano and Song (Didactic and Polemical): The Collected Writings of Clara Schumann's Father and Only Teacher*. Translated, edited, and annotated by Henry Pleasants. Stuyvesant, NY: Pendragon Press. First published as Wieck 1853.

Zimdars, Richard Louis, trans. and ed. 1996. *The Piano Master Classes of Franz Liszt, 1884–1886: Diary Notes of August Göllerich*. Edited by Wilhelm Jerger. Bloomington, Indiana University Press. First published 1975 as *Franz Liszts Klavierrunterricht von 1884–1886: dargestellt an den Tagebuchaufzeichnungen von August Göllerich*, edited by Wilhelm Jerger (Regensburg, Germany: Bosse).

VOCAL PATTERNS IN THE THEMES OF BERLIOZ'S INSTRUMENTAL MUSIC*

Jean-Pierre Bartoli

PARIS-SORBONNE UNIVERSITY

MELODY AND FORM

At the end of his *Memoirs*, Berlioz wrote one of the few passages in which he spoke openly about his own musical style. It is melody that he discusses first and on which he dwells the longest:

> It should be not difficult to recognize that although I may not actually confine myself to taking a short subject for the theme of a movement, as the greatest masters often did, I am always careful to make my compositions abundantly melodic. The value of these melodies, their distinction, originality and charm, may well be contested; it is not for me to estimate it. But to deny their existence is, I submit, dishonest or simply silly. Only, as they are often on a very large scale, a shallow, undeveloped sensibility is slow to grasp their form. They may also be combined with other subsidiary melodies which, for these same weak spirits, obscure their outline. Finally, such melodies are so unlike the desperately trivial little tunes which the riff-raff of the musical world understands by the term, that it cannot bring itself to admit they are tunes at all. The predominant features of my music are passionate expression, inward intensity, rhythmic impetus, and quality of unexpectedness. (Berlioz [1970] 1974, 588)

Here we notice first that Berlioz considers his art to be based essentially on this particular aspect of musical discourse. Melody and melodic development determine the musical flow and, eventually, the musical form. The latter is, therefore, the consequence of a melodic thought.

* This chapter is based on an article originally published in *Musurgia* (Bartoli 1997), but it develops the argument there in entirely new ways, especially regarding the influence of vocal styles.

We notice second that Berlioz draws no distinctions among the various musical genres in which he composed over the course of his career. His remarks are as pertinent to opera as to symphonies. In the very first sentence, he refers both to *melody* and to *theme*; and in his articles on Beethoven's symphonies, he even uses the term *song* (*chant*, in French). He uses the terms *idea*, *phrase*, *melody*, and *theme* (*idée*, *phrase*, *mélodie*, *theme*) almost as synonyms, with few differences in their connotations. Nevertheless, we must infer that *theme* implies a melodic material liable to be reworked, ornamented, developed; that is expressed very clearly in the first sentence. Thus, in commenting on the slow movement of Beethoven's Fifth Symphony in *A travers chants* he distinguishes between a "theme" in the first few bars that is open to many transformations and a "phrase" that remains unchanged throughout the movement (Berlioz 1994, 20).

In the *Memoirs*, quoted above, Berlioz makes it immediately clear that he takes particular care in the elaboration of interesting melodies. For him, this means the composition of unpredictable, extended melodies. (Later in the same passage he explicitly mentions "unexpectedness" as a salient feature of his style.) We may admire, in passing, his lucidity. He knows well what separates his themes from many by the "masters." The brevity and simplicity found in themes by the previous generation—which results, in the best instances, from a tremendous effort to elaborate thematic materials—astonishes him. He is attracted more by lyrical expansion than by concentration. Thus he is amazed at the banal character of the main theme of the first movement in Beethoven's First Symphony (Berlioz 1994, 11). Though acknowledging Beethoven's good example, he opposes it by using luxurious themes and melodies, frequently adding secondary ideas that make formal understanding more difficult.

We can draw four conclusions. First, Berlioz enjoins us not to behave like one of those "undeveloped sensibilities." We must keep our distance from the details of the score so that we can perceive the themes and the various melodic forms on a grand scale, in their entirety. The second conclusion is even more important: Berlioz does not seem to endorse the ideal of melodic concentration proclaimed by the three leading Viennese composers, who made an entire movement germinate from a thematic cell.

Third, Berlioz believes that any melody is capable of becoming a theme that is appropriate for symphonic development (an attribute that can be verified by experiment). He uses as thematic material not only ideas that can be easily germinated from cellular components but also whole melodies that are harder to split into motivic units. It is even possible that he sees no great difference between those categories. For this reason, I think it is inappropriate to differentiate between themes and "non-thematic" melodies in Berlioz's music: he himself made no distinction between them in either his writings or his scores. I shall therefore write interchangeably about "melodic" or "thematic" materials, and I shall use the words "theme" and "melody" equally.

Finally, Berlioz's comments cause one to wonder what sources influenced his personal approach to writing themes and melodies. My hypothesis is that vocal models are of predominant importance and that Berlioz simply doesn't think that composing for instruments can be usefully distinguished from composing for the voice.

MOTIVE CONSTRUCTION AND PERIODICITY IN THE VIENNESE INSTRUMENTAL STYLE

In both vocal and instrumental music, musicians of Mozart, Haydn and Beethoven's generation were naturally inclined towards four-bar phrases. For them, nothing was more obvious than to establish a regular and symmetrical periodicity by means of that four-unit entity, easily split into equal parts. However, exceptions to that rule are not unusual, particularly in more elaborate, "academic" genres (that is, in sonatas, symphonies, and *opera seria*, and even more in string quartets). They generally result from the composer's attempt to employ—or, rather, to search specifically for—a device to characterise his themes rhythmically in order to draw the audience's attention and interest.

It is not rare for a composer to return to the usual symmetric structure after the exposition of a theme that is not four bars long. That is the case in Mozart's sonatas K. 332, third movement, and K. 570, first movement; in both instances the first theme in the tonic does not evidence four-bar phrases, while the second is conventionally structured. The same thing occurs in Beethoven's First Symphony, in which the first theme of the initial allegro deliberately violates the four-bar principle, whereas the following secondary motive is strictly regular (see Rosen 1992).

The contrast between avoidance and affirmation of symmetrical structures in order to oppose a main theme with secondary thematic material also frequently occurs when the secondary tonality appears (for example, in sonata form). That is the case in Mozart's Sonatas K. 279, I; K. 283, I and especially II; K. 284, I; K. 285, I and III; K. 309, III; K. 311, I; K. 333, I; K. 457, II; and K. 576, I. It can also be found in Beethoven's Symphonies No. 1, II; No. 2, I; No. 4, IV; No. 7, II and IV; and No. 9, III. Finally, that opposition can frequently be noticed between a minuet or scherzo and its trio (for example, in five of the six scherzos in Haydn's op. 33 quartets) (see Bartoli 1994, 76).

In the Viennese school there is indeed a very close connection between periodicity and the motivic construction of themes. The principles of motivic elaboration were explicitly theorised in the second half of the eighteenth century, notably by Joseph Riepel and Heinrich Koch.[1] Here, however, we shall use Arnold Schoenberg's analytical vocabulary, which is inherited directly from that didactic and theoretical school but is modern enough to speak to us more clearly.

In his *Fundamentals of Musical Composition* (1967),[2] Schoenberg asserts that a well-constructed theme (a "sentence"

1. See Koch (1782–93, 3:226ff); an example from Koch is reprinted in Ratner (1980, 92–95), together with a discussion of both Koch and Riepel. See also Lester (1992).
2. Schoenberg's theory of musical phrase is grounded in a German tradition of form that is dominated by notions of coherence and organicism. In this context one might usefully read Marc Rigaudière's *La Théorie musicale germanique au XIXe siècle et l'idée de cohérence* (2009). The theoretical foundations of Schoenberg's approach to thematic construction in tonal music can be found in his *The Musical Idea and the Logic, Technique, and Art of Its Presentation* (Schoenberg 1995). It should be noted that when the first version of the present text was written, in 1991, the latter publication was not yet available. Schoenberg's *Fundamentals* is particularly relevant to the present discussion because of its analytical application of theoretical concepts. More recently, one finds a full treatment of Schoenberg as theoretician in Norton

or a "period") is based in its entirety on the development, through variation, of a limited number of basic "motive-forms." According to him, from the music of Haydn to that of Beethoven and his contemporaries, in practice motive development was usually organised around the repetition of motives in their initial form, together with transpositions and melodic variations. This is how, for example, the theme is built in the third movement of Beethoven's Piano Sonata op. 22 (figure 1).

Figure 1. Schoenberg's analysis of the theme of Beethoven's Piano Sonata, op. 22, third movement (Schoenberg 1967, 12)

Here the four-bar structure has been strictly respected. The same can be said of a great number of themes from the same period. However, motivic development of a theme can easily cause it

---

Dudeque's *Music Theory and Analysis in the Writings of Arnold Schoenberg* (2005), which contains a useful glossary of theoretical terms. Eighteenth-century phrase structure is extensively discussed in William E. Caplin's *Classical Form, a Theory of Formal Functions for the Instrumental Music of Haydn, Mozart, and Beethoven* (1998). This, too, was not available when the present text was first drafted. Caplin's modifications and refinements of Schoenberg's ideas do not fundamentally replace or alter my analysis of Berlioz's themes.

to overflow conventional limits. Thus the famous first theme of Mozart's G-Minor Symphony (No. 40) could very well have remained structured in four-bar units (bars 2–17) had it not been for the lengthening of the motive to create a cadential formula (bars 18–20). More instances, more daring still, certainly exist in Mozart's works. He was a master in rhythmic matters.

But some instances, both very representative and more radical than the example just given, can be found in Beethoven's music, particularly in his Fifth Symphony. There, the two main themes of the finale are structured in gradually expanding sections: the first theme in bars grouped 4+8 (= 4+4) +10 (= 4+2+4); the second with bars grouped 4+4+10. In both cases, it is the development of constituent motives that causes the phrases to grow and destroys any symmetry. So it is with the main themes of the third movement and both themes of the second movement. The main theme of the Sixth Symphony's first movement takes the principle of extension to an extreme, not without humour, in a structure of 4+4+4+4+16 (the last is all one unit). In every case, motivic repetition, with or without variation, is responsible for the rhythmic expansion.

In the second movement of the Fifth Symphony, the first theme deserves special attention: after the eight-bar exposition, the subdivision of which can be variously interpreted,[3] Beethoven adds a musical commentary with first a two-bar extension and then units of five, three, and four bars; the result is a completely asymmetrical theme that is twenty-two bars long. Moreover, the motivic structure of the initial eight bars is particularly free and can be subdivided in various ways; yet at the same time it is meticulously crafted from the first bar's constitutive cells. The development can actually be reduced to successive variations on the initial thematic fragment, as if it were being progressively refined. The freedom and ambiguity within the conventional eight-bar frame results from a motivic development emancipated from any metrical restraints. In this case, then, the motivic struc-

3. In the first book of his *Cours de composition musicale*, Vincent d'Indy (1912, 41) refuses all subdivisions and views the whole as one "phrase" made from a single "period."

ture shapes the rhythm of the musical phrase and thus becomes the cause of its regularity (figure 2).

Figure 2. Beethoven, Fifth Symphony, second movement, main theme, motivic elaboration

MOTIVIC CONSTRUCTION AND PERIODICITY IN VOCAL MUSIC BEFORE BERLIOZ: THE MUSICAL STROPHE

Let us now turn to some examples of vocal music. We shall start from the most common and simple models, the first that Berlioz heard at the Côte Saint-André during his youth, as he recalled in his memoirs: the French romances.

I opened a miscellany from the Napoleonic era and examined about twenty romances to study their periodicity. Reading that very prolific, very widely distributed music enables one to conclude that regular bar structures were extremely frequent. A great many romances are exclusively and entirely built of four or five phrases divided into four bars each. But we can also frequently observe an expansion of the four-bar unit. This expansion is generally linked to melodic development and an intensified expression: a kind of climax, as it were. I propose to consider a few very clear examples.

The first one (figure 3) is by Louis Sejan: "Le jardinier fleuriste" (note how closely the theme resembles the finale of Mozart's Concerto No. 25 and also "La Marseillaise").

Figure 3. Louis Sejan, "Le jardinier fleuriste," first strophe (Sejan 1813, 4–5)

Everything seems to be constituted in four-bar units; an initial period of 4+4 bars is followed by a four-bar commentary and then a conclusion in 4+6 bars (see table 1). But the final six bars cannot be divided; they result from lengthened note values in the melody, which reaches its climax shortly before the last cadence. It is the position of the climax that brings about the extension of the musical phrase and, consequently, the break from regular four-bar units. (Actually, this is a very typical device when a climactic phrase is repeated, seen in much vocally inspired instrumental music, such as Mendelssohn's *Lieder ohne Worte*).

a1	a2	b	c1	c2
antecedent	consequent	commentary	1st conclusion 1st climax	2nd conclusion 2nd climax
4	4	4	4	6

Table 1. Structure of Sejan's strophe

Not infrequently, an extension of a structural unit occurs in a contrasting phrase that usually follows the theme itself. In instrumental music that is in binary form, this often happens just after the first double bar line. In this case, the extension is occasioned by a brief sequential development or the preparation of the half-cadence. The same device can also be found in romances. The sequences are usually two bars long; thus, commonly, in such cases, a four-bar unit is followed by a two-bar unit or a succession of three two-bar units.

These two locations (just after the theme and in the final climax) can both contain extensions in a single romance. This can be illustrated with a "big hit" from the pre-Berlioz era: the aria "Nel cor più non mi sento" from Paisiello's *La Molinara* (1788, performed in Paris the following year; figure 4).

Figure 4. Giovanni Paisiello, "Nel cor piu non me sento," first strophe (Paisiello, n.d.)

This strophic aria is written in "romance" style. I happened upon it in the same miscellany that contained the Sejan. Beethoven wrote a series of variations on it. It follows a ternary form, a–a′–b–(a), that is very common in nineteenth-century Italian arias. In this case (table 2), as in the Sejan romance, the initial regular period is extended to six bars (4+2) at the end of the strophe. But the phrase before also contains an extension leading to a half cadence. Since there are only four phrases instead of five, the two prolonged units are conjoined.

a1	a2	b	a3 (development of a)
antecedent	consequent	commentary fonte + half cadence; fermata climax	conclusion perfect cadence (2nd climax)
4	4	6 (4+2)	6 (4+2)

Table 2. Structure of Paisiello's strophic aria

"Ô mon amante, ma Zélie" (figure 5), a pretty romance by Boieldieu, also contains both types of extensions, though here they are separated, since the strophe contains five musical phrases. The commentary, which modulates to the relative major, repeats the cadence, creating two added bars; then, after four bars above a tonic pedal, the concluding phrase is extended to six bars (table 3). Whereas the first six-bar phrase is clearly 4+2, the last one, which includes the climax, is in fact the conjunction of two units (4+3 bars), with an elision that permits the fourth bar of the first unit to serve also as the first bar of the following one.

Ô mon a-
man - te_ma Zé - li - e c'en est fait_ je vais te quit - ter loin de ta
pp
pré - sen - ce ché - ri - e Le vais es-sa- yer_ d'e-xis - ter Ces
chants que la dou-leur m'ins - pi - re te rap-pe - le - ront mes tour -

Figure 5. François-Adrien Boieldieu, "Ô mon amante, ma Zélie," first strophe (Boieldieu [1797])

a1	a2	b	c	d
antecedent	consequent	commentary	prolongation	provisional conclusion & final conclusion
		in relative major	tonic pedal	climax
4	4	6 (4+2)	4 (2+2)	6 (4+3 with elision)

Table 3. Structure of Boieldieu's strophe

Even pieces from more sophisticated repertoires are based on this structure whenever they refer to the style of a "romance." "Sombre forêt," the very famous romance sung by Mathilde in Rossini's *Guillaume Tell* (1829), uses a five-phrase structure (table 4). Yet what we hear in the first stanza is an initial group of four regular four-bar phrases that is followed by a very extended

First stanza

a	a'	a"	a'''	coda
				vocalise
I	V	sequence	conclusion	climax and conclusion
4	4	4	4	11 (1 orchestral + 10)

Second stanza

a	a'	a"	a'''	coda		
				1st vocalise	2nd vocalise	3rd vocalise
I	V	sequence	conclusion	climax & conclusion 1	conclusion 2	fermata
4	4	4	4	11 (1+10)	10	2 (elision) + 6 (orchestra)

Table 4. Structure of Mathilde's aria ("Sombre forêt") in Rossini's *Guillaume Tell*

ten-bar coda, for stylistic reasons. In the second stanza, Rossini extends the principle still further, thus transferring this romance into the realm of Italian coloratura arias. The four-bar units overflow because of the climaxes in these two codas.

Returning to the Viennese repertoire and leaving the romance, we can note a similar structure in "Porgi amor," the countess's cavatina in Mozart's *Le Nozze di Figaro*. After the first two four-bar phrases, the lyric and melodic development brings about an elongation of the musical units and a reduced sense of regular bar structures. The very end, through an innate sense of balance, returns to a simple four-bar phrase (table 5). Obviously, as was the case previously for the romances, the harmonic progression is closely linked to the phrase structure. Still, it is the melodic development that seems to be the determining compositional factor.

a	a'	b		c		coda
		orchestra / voice	and fermata			
					perfect cadence	
		9 (4x3 elided)+2		5 (elided)+3+2		
4	4	11		10		4

Table 5. Structure of the Countess's cavatina ("Porgi amor") in *Le Nozze di Figaro*, beginning with the soprano's entry

Whereas the prosody for tragic or noble characters is supple and even eccentric, secondary, more common characters sing in a more straightforward style. For example, Kaspar's tragic aria in Weber's *Der Freischütz* ("Schweig, Schweig"), which ends the first act, is written in a parlando style with asymmetrical periods (3+3+10+7, etc.). In contrast, Ännchen's "Kommt ein schlanker Bursch gegangen," near the beginning of the second act, is written in a more popular vein and is structured with almost no exceptions in strict four-bar units (orchestra 4+4; voice 4+4+4+3 [elided], 4+4+4+4, etc.). In the same Singspiel, the honest and pure Agatha sings the famous cantabile aria "Leise, leise fromme Weise"; this, too, manifests four-bar regularity: 4+4; 4+4; 3 (orchestra); 4+4; 4+4. Even the theme of the stretta that ends this aria, though on the whole more "free," remains basically symmetric.

This natural respect for four-bar structures can also be found in most of Schubert's lieder. Some of them, in strict four-bar units, are written in a simple style reminiscent of the romance: "Das Wandern," which opens the cycle *Die schöne Müllerin*, or "Die Forelle," for example. Others are masterfully complex and elaborate. In "An die Musik," for example, there are uncanny overlaps of the vocal and piano lines and, above all, an ambiguous first bar in every strophe that can be viewed both as the opening of the phrase and as a long anacrusis. Thus one can represent the structure of this lied in two different ways (see table 6): the first one includes the initial bar in the period, while the second one treats it as an anacrusis.

	rit (a)	a1	a2		b	c	rit.
voice		3	3	0	4	5 (3+2)	
piano	3	4	4		4	5	4
						climax	

	rit (a)	a1		a2			b	c	rit.
voice	0 *an*	3	0 *an*	2	0	*an*	3	5 (3+2)	
piano	*an* 2	3	5			4		5	4
								climax	

Table 6. Structure of Schubert's "An die Musik," two versions (*an* signifies "anacrusis")

Beyond the elegant flexibility with which it contradicts the principles of the four-bar structure, "An die Musik" also claims one's attention when, shortly before the final cadence, the phrase again expands in moving towards its expressive climax. The lyrical expansion that we have observed in a variety of examples seems indeed to be characteristic of vocal writing.

In sum, for the Viennese composers and their contemporaries, symmetrical periodicity was a natural component of musical style, precisely in order that it be expressively contradicted. This they did with, for the best among them, incomparable finesse. However, this even, symmetrical periodicity appears to be still more natural in instrumental music (influenced, as it can be, by rhythmic models taken from dance) than in vocal music (which is influenced by another rhythmic model—the prosody of language, by its nature uneven and asymmetrical despite poetic metres). We can also observe that in instrumental music, motivic development is necessarily the main motivation for extensions to the bar structure. That can also be true for vocal music; but in this case, more commonly, the causes of this phenomenon are found in the unfolding vocal line, the accentuation, the lengthened note values, or the incorporation of coloratura passages.

FROM VOCAL TO INSTRUMENTAL: LATE BEETHOVEN

It would seem that the further Beethoven went in his creative career, the more he tried to free his music from conventional four-bar patterns. The structure of several arias from *Fidelio*, which was composed during his middle creative period (1805–14), is noticeably less periodic than the structures of the instrumental examples discussed above. Comparing *Der Freischütz* to *Fidelio*, one is struck by the extent to which Beethoven refuses to be tempted by blatant four-bar phrases even in arias that are written in a simple, Singspiel style. In the first part of Florestan's aria ("In des Lebens Frülingstagen"), for example, the structure is 5+5+5+4+5+6; and the first part of Leonore's aria ("Komm, Hoffnung, lass den letzten Stern") is even more complex (table 7).

orch.	voice							
	a	b	c				d	
				diminutions			*messa di voce*	
4	4	4	5	+	3	+ 2	10 (3+7)	+ 4
					climax 1		climax 2	

Table 7. Structure of Leonore's aria ("Komm, Hoffnung, lass den letzten Stern") in *Fidelio*

Quite possibly the increased use of such free models in vocal writing might be, in part, responsible for the freedom of Beethoven's instrumental writing towards the end of his career. In the adagio cantabile from the Ninth Symphony (figure 6), for example, the repetition by the woodwinds of the last notes of each violin phrase creates a subtle ease in the rhythm, giving the impression that time has been suspended. The effect is emphasised because the woodwind and string parts overlap, so that silences arising from breathing are hidden; if the woodwind parts are removed, one hears a regular four-bar structure. In addition, the motivic construction of this theme is harder to perceive than in the excerpt from the Fifth Symphony discussed earlier.

In this passage the network of constituent motives (the fourth that runs through the whole symphony, filled-in melodic thirds, and dotted rhythmic motives) offers at the same time more flexibility and more diversity and above all is half-hidden behind surface features. The vocal qualities are obvious; yet the rhythmic structure is not as bold as the ones used in *Fidelio*.

The same remarks apply to the late sonatas: a four-bar structure remains perceptible even in the most cantabile movements. The first theme in the slow movement from the "Hammerklavier" displays four-bar structures that, though hardly perceptible when well performed, are nonetheless real. There are in fact five four-bar units, followed by a solitary last one that stretches to five bars: what results is highly uneven indeed since, instead of the traditional sixteen bars, we have here a much enlarged section containing twenty-one bars (including the famous initial bar added by Beethoven after the first draft). Most themes from op. 109 display four-bar structures, and even the "Klagende Gesang" from op. 110 conforms strictly to the four-unit principle. On the other hand, the last quartets are more adventurous and come close to the free construction of the *Fidelio* arias we have just examined. This is especially obvious in Quartet No. 15: the first main theme that is strictly and fully in four-bar units doesn't appear until the introduction to the finale and the finale theme itself. It is clear that vocal patterns have influenced the writing of these late quartets.

Figure 6. Beethoven, Ninth Symphony, third movement, adagio cantabile.

PERIODICITY IN BERLIOZ THEMES

It is important to study Beethoven's works at length, since they ranked among Berlioz's favourites. They influenced him a great deal in developing his own style. Berlioz, in fact, expressed his own views about four-bar structures and periodicity in a "feuilletons" written in 1837. As usual an enemy of convention, he rejects the idea, widespread in academic teaching, that regular melodic periods are necessary:

> Most musicians recognize as properly cast in rhythm only those melodies whose phrases they call "square," that is, which contain four or eight measures each and end on a strong beat. They do not seem aware that true "squareness" is simply symmetry, and that a given phrase whose first member consists of three or five measures may be regular by reason of the comparable member with which it concludes, making a total of six measures or of ten. No one will admit, either, that the non-parity or, if you will, the irregularity of certain rhythmic units is precisely what in certain cases produces force or liveliness of expression. (Berlioz 1837, [2], as translated in Barzun 1969, 2:337)[4]

Drawing inspiration from this text and taking it as a point of departure, it is thus possible to distinguish, with respect to rhythm and phrasing, two categories of material:

(a) Regular rhythmic structures: that is, sections that possess symmetrical correspondence and that manifest balanced rhythmic proportions. These are classic four-bar structures to which any other symmetrical structure based on sections having an even number of bars or beats can be added. There are actually two types of such structures: those that are

4. "La plupart des amateurs et des artistes ne reconnaissent encore de mélodies régulièrement rythmées que celles dont les phrases sont ce qu'ils appellent *carrées*, c'est-à-dire formées de quatre ou huit mesures, et qui finissent sur un *temps fort*. Ils paraissent ignorer que la véritable carrure est simplement la symétrie, et que telle phrase, dont le premier membre se compose de trois ou de cinq mesures, est régulière à cause du membre correspondant qui la termine, en lui donnant une totalité de six mesures ou de dix. On se refuse également à avouer que l'imparité ou, si l'on veut, l'irrégularité de certaines coupes rythmiques, est précisément quelquefois ce qui fait leur force et leur vivacité d'expression."

completely regular throughout; and others that are initially regular but contain a later amplified, or rather developed, section that is not always regular.

(b) Irregular rhythmic structures: that is, all those that do not fit in the first category.

Table 8 summarises the categories that thus can be found in Berlioz's works.

A: Regular structures, according to Berlioz	A1.	Four-bar regular phrases in two or four sections
	A2.	Two four-bar initial units followed by a development section
	A3.	Regular and symmetrical structures but not in four-bar units
	A4.	Regular structures, not in four-bar units and with uneven sections
B: Irregular structures, according to Berlioz	B1.	"False" irregular structures
	B2.	Structures in which one unit is unequal to the others
	B3.	An initial four-bar unit is followed by irregular units
	B4.	Structures that are wholly irregular

Table 8. Categories of periodic structures according to Berlioz

I have elsewhere studied over a hundred themes in Berlioz's instrumental music, including almost all the composer's main thematic ideas in symphonic music (Bartoli 1991, chap. 6). Of 107 themes studied, 24 are type A1 and nearly as many (20) are type A2. There are 14 themes of type A3, and five of type A4. In seven cases the structure could have been regular but was deliberately made irregular by Berlioz ("false" irregularity, type B1). Thirty-eight structures are absolutely irregular (types B2, 3, 4).

If we apply theoretical texts from Berlioz's time, most of which asserted that the only structures that can be called regular are those that conform to the four-bar principle, we find there are about forty regular themes, of which only twenty adhere strictly to four-bar units throughout, and about sixty that are irregular. However, applying Berlioz's categories, discussed above, the conclusions are wholly reversed. About sixty themes become regular, and about forty remain irregular. This last figure is impressive: for what other composers born between 1800 and 1810 are the proportions comparable? The only way to answer this intrinsically stylistic question would be to apply the same statistical experiment to Berlioz's contemporaries. You will understand if I leave the question unanswered. But when one studies, for instance, the rhythmic units in Schumann's *Kreisleriana*, it is perhaps surprising to find that four-bar structures are nearly omnipresent. It thus becomes important, first of all, to grasp why Berlioz prefers irregular structures and, second, to determine the most remarkable type of irregularity.

A synthesis of these results reveals that Berlioz preferred to build melodies and thematic structures from regular units at the start and then to extend them in the sections that follow, just like in the vocal melodies described above. The emotional and structural weight shifts, then, to the last sections, which usually include insistent, often varied, motivic repetitions. This is particularly noticeable in melodies of type B3, which contains the largest number of irregular patterns. Many of those themes sound typically "Berliozian" (regardless of tempo), and yet the same could be said about the examples above that are drawn from Beethoven's works. Is it safe, then, to assume a clear influence of the great master on his younger colleague?

MOTIVIC CONSTRUCTION AND PERIODICITY IN BERLIOZ'S MUSIC

Very few of Berlioz's themes are built strictly from a simple generative motive. Constructions such as those found in the main themes from Beethoven's Fifth and Third Symphonies or in Brahms's later Fourth Symphony (in which the interval of the third permeates the whole of the first theme) are notable exceptions for Berlioz, to such an extent that those themes don't even seem to be entirely his. Rossini could have put his name to the secondary theme from the *Francs-Juges* overture, which is based on a single rhythmic motive; in the first movement of *Harold en Italie* the main secondary theme could be by, for example, Weber. In the "Marche des pèlerins" from the same work, Berlioz turns to monothematism in a very obsessive way, but for a different purpose: to imitate a liturgical incantation, remote indeed from the symphonic style.

Themes based on two motives, or more generally two opposed ideas, are more frequent. They show Berlioz conforming to the standards of his time. This is often the method of composition of "periods," as Schoenberg (1967, 20–21) called them, or of any melody using symmetrical antecedents and consequents (that is, in category A1 or A3, above).

However, Berlioz uses generative motives in a more original way in the elaboration of his more personal, more irregular themes. The originality lies in the liberties taken; motives become distorted in several ways, melodic as well rhythmic. The affinities between different motivic alternatives are in fact hard to describe; their relationship to the initial model is tenuous and seemingly irrational. Thus the second theme of the overture to *Benvenuto Cellini* (beginning at bar 42) starts with two motive forms that seem quite different but which are very similar on an underlying level (see figure 7, second staff). The subsequent bars return to the rhythmic pattern from the second bar and then seem to escape into a long cantilena in which "Viennese" motivic development, at first hearing, seems to be absent. Yet the melodic contour in bars 10 to 11, and even more in 12 to 14, recalls the extended curve underlying bars 5 to 10 (figure 7, third staff). An even more remote link occurs in the final section (bars 15 to 17, then 18 to 23), which could recall the very beginning of this theme. It is, however, difficult to demonstrate this conclusively; there are only indications, such as the recurring intervals of fifths and fourths (fourth staff), a possible return of the underlying motive from the initial bars (second staff), and an underlying descending line in bars 18 to 23 (b–a–a–g–f♯–e; then c–b–a–g, inspired by the d–c–b–a–g–f♯ from the first four bars). (These descending lines are indicated by the unslurred noteheads on the third staff of figure 7.)

Figure 7. Berlioz, Overture, *Benvenuto Cellini*, slow introduction, second theme

An interesting comparison can be made between this theme and that of the adagio from Beethoven's Ninth Symphony. They seem to be linked in both their flexibility and their vocality; yet in Berlioz's theme, except for the first phrase, a structure based on four-bar units is certainly not fundamental to the idea, whereas such a structure is clearly evident in Beethoven's melody. Moreover, in Berlioz's theme can be found similarities in melodic contour that can be justified only by accepting less precise intervallic relations. Finally, another contrast is evident in Berlioz's greater diversity of rhythmic values: in this, Berlioz's theme is less motivically coherent than the theme from Beethoven's Ninth and is instead much closer to the singing style of the *Fidelio* arias.

This theme looks like a strophe from a very elaborate romance—which would not come as a surprise to connoisseurs of Berlioz: it is used again later in the opera, not sung but again played by the English horn, in the "Ariette d'Arlequin" during the King Midas pantomime. This theme turns out to be an imitation of an aria heard at a theatrical fête, a favourite setting for romance; as such, it represents pure melodic inspiration.

THE GRADUAL EMERGENCE OF A MOTIVIC DEVELOPMENT SECTION

The so-called "Viennese" norm usually entails the development of motives that are derived from the initial portion of the theme. That was the case in the Beethoven examples above: motives to be developed appear as early as the first or the second bar, and at any rate within the first full statement. However, although the theme from the Ninth Symphony (figure 6) complies with this rule, it also progressively introduces a rhythmic motive—two or three quavers followed by a dotted crotchet, quaver, and crotchet—which hadn't been present at the start. It appears only at bar 9 and eventually replaces the material heard in bar 2, from which it was derived. By the end, it is repeated almost obsessively: nothing else can be heard.

This passage, then, sets out a method for constructing material that is rather unusual for symphonic repertoire, but not at all unusual in vocal music. The melody progresses linearly, as if the composer was guided by the prosody of a text to be set to music. Each section seems to give birth to the next one; and the echoing woodwinds accentuate this effect, especially since they act something like an accompanying instrument. All this, which serves to underline the final cadence and its preparation by an expressive climax created through motivic development, seems to be borrowed from a vocal style. This approach seems to me more typical of vocal strophes than of instrumental themes. Not without justification is this movement called *adagio cantabile*.

Of course, this motivic development, which appears as the melody is unfolding, is intrinsically linked to the way that

Figure 8. Berlioz, *Symphonie fantastique,* first movement, *"idée fixe."*

four-bar units are enlarged both in simple romances and in more complex arias, as was demonstrated above. In Beethoven's Ninth, as in most Berlioz themes, a four-bar structure is still perceptible in the first few phrases; then, as the climax approaches, motivic development causes a metric extension in the last phrases.

The "*idée fixe*" from the *Symphonie fantastique*, as presented in the first movement (figure 8), develops not from the first motive, though that is structurally very significant both rhythmically and melodically, but rather from the ascending semitone that follows and the conjunct descending line that comes next. In *The Romantic Generation*, Charles Rosen (1995, 547–50) critiques Edward T. Cone's rhythmic analysis[5] and demonstrates that this theme actually demonstrates an underlying four-bar regularity that is hidden by repositioning phrases in relation to strong or weak beats. One only has to sing this theme while beating an unvarying four counts (one per bar) to understand what Rosen means. Still, this feeling of regularity can be utterly annihilated if the performers choose to accentuate according to the melodic shape rather than in steady units of four. (This is a central point in Rosen's commentary.) By indicating no accentuation, Berlioz gives performers total license to do this. Consequently, one might argue that this theme is not really in four-bar units; it is a series of phrases of unequal length: 8+7+(4+4+4+5)+9. In fact, both analyses are correct: Berlioz seeks here a supple and disconcerting ambiguity (as Rosen justly remarks) with, above all, a kind of melodic rubato that is captured rhythmically in the score.

The main theme from the third movement of the same symphony also develops a motive that is not significant at the start (figure 9).

5. For which, see Cone (1971, especially 254).

Figure 9. Berlioz, *Symphonie fantastique,* third movement, first theme

Such constructions are not at all unusual in Berlioz's music. At some unpredictable point in the melodic development, he seems to grasp "on the wing" a melodic cell, sometimes trivial, that he can treat as a thematic motive. He manages to draw from it some unsuspected interest, using for that purpose a number of variations and repetitions. Thus, he puts in motion an important process in which he expands the musical phrase. The theme then moves inexorably towards an expressive climax in which its form culminates, a process that is comparable to the progression toward a climax in a vocal strophe.

Figure 10. Berlioz, *Benvenuto Cellini,* overture: Allegro, main theme

It would be good to analyse these many expanding thematic and melodic structures one by one, but space does not permit it. I shall merely mention a few more examples that are representative. The main theme from the overture to *Benvenuto Cellini* (figure 10), compact and quick, would appear to be regular. Nevertheless, one can still hear a very disturbing first section in which the strong beats are displaced with respect to the metre and a drive to a final climax that conceals the rhythmic regularity. Thus, although each section of figure 10 is four bars long, the beats are not perceptible in s1, s3 follows s2 without interruption, s4 ends with a silent measure, and the harmonic rhythm is very capricious.

In the central theme from the *Roméo et Juliette* adagio (figure 11), Berlioz could have composed an initial four-bar phrase simply by remaining in the key of f♯ minor. Instead, he writes a six-bar unit (seven bars if the first note is not regarded as an anacrusis) with a supple and unexpected ending, no doubt motivated by the modulation to A major, which itself is accomplished in an unusual way (a plagal cadence). One might expect an equally long consequent. Instead, Berlioz prefers to shorten the melody to end after five bars, even though he has just broadened the rhythmic values in a sort of written rallentando (in the third bar of the consequent); and then he simply repeats the final three bars, by way of extension. Such exceptional melodic flexibility seems to be dictated by an unheard text.

The theme, as such, ends here. But Berlioz adds a codetta, which develops the same motivic ending instead of the motives from the beginning. The melody seems to want not to end; the composer was apparently reluctant to leave it. The reason is understandable: this theme represents Juliet.

Figure 11. Berlioz, *Roméo et Juliette,* adagio, second theme

In the same symphony, the fugue subject for Juliet's funeral procession very clearly insists on developing the concluding motivic idea, chromatic and plaintive (figure 12). This subject, with a very asymmetrical rhythm, unfolds with no regard for the time signature.

Figure 12. Berlioz, *Roméo et Juliette,* fugue subject from "Convoi funèbre"

One could cite many more examples of the same type: the ball theme from *Roméo et Juliette*, the theme from the slow introduction to the overture *Le corsaire*, its equivalent in the *Béatrice et Bénédict* overture, the main theme from the finale to *Harold en Italie*, and so on. But I shall conclude with the main theme from the first movement of the largely unknown, somewhat Mahlerian *Symphonie funèbre et triomphale* (figure 13).

Figure 13. Berlioz, *Symphonie funèbre et triomphale*, first movement, first theme

This is built primarily from a dotted-rhythm motive, introduced as early as the second bar, but the motivic development is increasingly devoted to an offshoot whose outlines come into clearer view between bars 9 and 11. Berlioz devotes the rest of his theme to a sequential treatment of this motive, which leads to a strongly marked expressive climax.

Julian Rushton (1983, 145–46) explained perfectly the process that generates this theme's dynamic impulse.[6] If Berlioz had so wished, he could have concluded the theme by remaining in A flat at bar 8. Instead, the consequent is interrupted by a diminished seventh, which imperatively demands a continuation. Bar 9 returns not to the initial motive but to the rhythm of bar 3, and the anacrusis at the end of bar 10 employs a rhythm hitherto reserved for second beats. The extensive development that follows is launched by this dotted rhythm. The resulting

6. In a general way, the chapter on "Melody" in Rushton's noteworthy study (1983, 144–67) explores ideas that are very similar to the present chapter. The two must be regarded as complementary: the models put forth by Rushton to describe Berlioz's melodic constructions are somewhat different from those presented here, but in both cases the origin is ultimately vocal. For Rushton, the primary source is Gluck; my chapter focuses more on the romance repertoire and late Beethoven.

theme, which could have been presented in only eight bars, thus requires twenty (4+4+2+10).

With this instance, Berlioz draws closer to Beethoven's late style, clearly departing from Beethoven's second creative period. It can even be said that, by using this technique, Berlioz distinguishes himself from the composers of the previous generation. What was for Beethoven an experiment, a calculated effect, an attempt at innovation at the end of his compositional career, has become for Berlioz a personal, stylistic norm.

A comparison of these several examples makes it clear that most motivic developments, placed at the end of extended themes, gradually reduce a basic motive to a few notes, after which it disappears. Accents become more and more numerous and closely placed, annihilating any periodic regularity and contradicting the metric stresses indicated by the time signature. Thus these themes are characterised by a truly theatrical (or, more generally, discursive) vitality, which makes of them a kind of narrative tale or abridged drama.

Once the basic material has been established, the musical discourse builds inexorably from a newly introduced element to a climax (which can be tragic, as in the *Symphonie funèbre*, or ecstatic, as in the *Benvenuto Cellini* overture). The climax then leads rapidly to a conclusion. This formal design could be summarised in the scheme below, to which the classical elements of Greek tragedy have been added:

(1) Exposition of the first thematic elements (prologue)
(2) Introduction of a new motivic element (peripeteia)
(3) Intensification by means of motivic development (desis)
(4) Climax (main pathetic event, pathos)
(5) Resolution (denouement, lysis)

Many themes from Berlioz's symphonic works are thus like strophes, short closed forms as in vocal music, already laden with expressive weight and containing an inner drama. Because of this, his most personal themes contain an undeniable narrative value; and it is this that makes him an innovator. If, indeed, he was encouraged by the example of Beethoven to adopt vocal melodic writing to symphonic music, he carried the experiment further. Beethoven kept those experiments for precise occasions (like slow and cantabile movements), whereas Berlioz used them in every part of his symphonic forms. Thus, he managed to build up thematic and melodic structures that were for the time astonishingly free.

Yet, in so doing, he turned his back on the German symphonic tradition, albeit perhaps unconsciously. Ultimately, the construction of the theme from the *Symphonie funèbre et triomphale* is more like that of Bellini's aria "Casta diva" than a theme from any Beethoven symphony. In both contexts, of course, the construction of a theme requires development of its motivic constituents. However, composers in the Viennese tradition didn't explore all the potential motivic developments at once; they held some resources in reserve for the rest of the movement. Berlioz, in contrast, pours everything in immediately, inserting within the themes themselves motivic variations usually saved for later. This is why Berlioz's symphonic themes end up looking and sounding like vocal music. This is also why Berlioz so frequently reused melodies that were originally vocal, turning them into symphonic themes.

However, by thus resorting in symphonies or overtures to thematic constructions that don't belong to a traditional symphonic style, he cut the ground from under his own feet. Whereas the Viennese (and their contemporaries and successors) saved their ammunition, Berlioz frequently exhausted all the motivic possibilities of his thematic ideas as soon as he found them. And after hearing a theme that contains all its development from the start, everything seems to have been said.

One thinks of La Fontaine's fable of the grasshopper and the ant. After having used what I would call "the grasshopper technique"—that is, after he had spontaneously, freely, and generously sung "all the summer long"—Berlioz was faced with the need for a fresh impulse in his musical discourse. How would he proceed now that "winter" had come—a "winter" that, in symphonic forms, has to contain thematic development? How would he manage to get out of the trap he had set for himself?

By thus raising the problem of symphonic form in Berlioz's music, we understand that he had no choice but to become formally innovative. And so he was—and very brilliantly, too. But that is another story, for another time. . . .

REFERENCES

Bartoli, Jean-Pierre. 1991. *L'œuvre symphonique de Berlioz: Forme et principes de développement*. PhD thesis, Paris-Sorbonne University (Paris IV).

———. 1994. "Une Introduction à l'analyse des Quatuors op. 33 de Haydn." In *Préparation aux épreuves d'analyse musicale*, 67–88. Paris: Editions Eska.

———. 1997. "La 'Technique de la cigale': la construction périodique et motivique des thèmes de Berlioz." *Musurgia* 4(2): 59–76.

Barzun, Jacques. 1969. *Berlioz and the Romantic Century*. 3rd ed. 2 vols. New York: Columbia University Press.

Berlioz, Hector. 1837. "Strauss. Son orchestre, ses valses.—De l'avenir du rhythme." *Journal des débats politiques et littéraires*, 10 November, [1]–[2].

———. (1970) 1974. *The Memoirs of Hector Berlioz Including His Travels in Italy, Germany, Russia and England, 1803–1865*. Translated and edited by David Cairns. Rev. ed. St Albans, UK: Panther Books. First published 1865 as *Mémoires de Hector Berlioz, comprenant ses voyages en Italie, en Allemagne, en Russie et en Angleterre, 1803–1865* (Paris: for the author). This translation first published 1969 (London: Victor Gollancz); rev. ed. first published 1970 (St. Albans: Panther Books).

———. 1994. *The Art of Music and Other Essays*. Edited and translated by Elizabeth Csicsery-Rónay. Bloomington, IN: Indiana University Press. First published as 1862 as *A travers chants: Etudes musicales, adorations boutades et critiques* (Paris: Michel Lévy). The translation based on the edition by Léon Guichard (Paris: Gründ, 1971).

Boieldieu, François-Adrien. [1797.] "Ô mon amante, ma Zélie." *La Muse du jour* 1(26), n.p.

Caplin, William E. 1998. *Classical Form: A Theory of Formal Functions for the Instrumental Music of Haydn, Mozart, and Beethoven*. New York: Oxford University Press.

Cone, Edward T. 1971. "Schumann Amplified: An Analysis." In *Hector Berlioz: Fantastic Symphony: An Authoritative Score, Historical*

Background, Analysis, Views and Comments, edited by Edward T. Cone, 249–77. New York: W. W. Norton.

Dudeque, Norton. 2005. *Music Theory and Analysis in the Writings of Arnold Schoenberg (1874–1951)*. Aldershot, UK: Ashgate.

Indy, Vincent d'. 1912. *Cours de composition musicale. Premier livre.* With the collaboration of Auguste Sérieyx. Paris: Durand. Translated and edited by Gail Hilson Woldu as *Course in Musical Composition* (Norman: University of Oklahoma Press, 2010).

Koch, Heinrich Christoph. 1782–93. *Versuch einer Anleitung zur composition.* 3 vols. Leipzig: Adam Friedrich Böhme.

Lester, Joel. 1992. *Compositional Theory in the Eighteenth Century.* Cambridge, MA: Harvard University Press.

Paisiello, Giovanni. n.d. *La Molinara.* "Nel cor piu non mi sento." Chanté par Mmes Festa et Maffei et M. Garcia, arrangé avec accompagnement de piano par Pacini. Paris: Chez Jouve.

Ratner, Leonard G. 1980. *Classic Music, Expression, Form and Style.* New York: Schirmer.

Rigaudière, Marc. 2009. *La théorie musicale germanique au XIXe siècle et l'idée de cohérence.* Paris: Société française de musicologie.

Rosen, Charles. 1992. "Variations sur le principe de la carrure: Périodicité rythmique et accentuation à l'époque romantique." *Analyse musicale* 29 (November): 96–106.

———. 1995. *The Romantic Generation.* Cambridge, MA: Harvard University Press.

Rushton, Julian. 1983. *The Musical Language of Berlioz.* Cambridge: Cambridge University Press.

Schoenberg, Arnold. 1967. *Fundamentals of Musical Composition.* Edited by Gerald Strang and Leonard Stein. London: Faber and Faber.

———. 1995. *The Musical Idea and the Logic, Technique, and Art of Its Presentation.* Translated by Patricia Carpenter and Severine Neff. New York: Columbia University Press. Transcription and English translation of an unfinished manuscript written 1934–36.

Sejan, Louis. 1813. "Le jardinier fleuriste," paroles de M. ***. In *Trois romances*, 4–5. Paris: Bureau du Journal des Arts.

PLOT AND NARRATIVE IN MENDELSSOHN'S CHAMBER MUSIC FOR STRINGS AND PIANO

Douglass Seaton

The Florida State University

BACKGROUND CONSIDERATIONS: APPROACHING MUSICAL NARRATOLOGY

Two of my interests over a number of years have been Mendelssohn's works and the application of narrative theory to nineteenth-century music. The invitation to contribute to this symposium therefore suggested a particular challenge—to apply a narratological approach to some of Mendelssohn's compositions. In order to explore the limits of narratology as a critical method, I have chosen to examine some of the least likely prospects for such a project: selected movements from Mendelssohn's chamber music for piano and strings. Three of these works represent the composer in the beginning of his career and stand at the early boundary of the period in which we might expect to observe narrativity in operation. None of them bears any explicit programme or other literary connection.

We cannot take for granted the viability of narratology as a musicological method. One of the most sceptical critics of its possibilities, Jean-Jacques Nattiez (1990), has argued that listeners could identify narrativity only by inventing their own stories to correspond to musical event-sequences, stories that might have nothing to do with the intentions of the music itself, thus calling into question the idea that narrative in music consists of anything more than a sort of solipsistic self-indulgence by naïve listeners. One thinks here of the "keys" to Beethoven's music offered by Arnold Schering (1934, [1936] 1973), imaginative but entirely made-up programmes for instrumental works. Peter Kivy (2002, 135–59) objects to the claim that music can be narrative on the grounds that he finds it impossible to reconcile the inherent use of repetitions in common musical forms with the absurdity of such repetitions in a story.[1] Carolyn Abbate (1989) questions the existence of narrative in music because music has no past tense, which means that it can only operate as events taking place in the present and not as actions reported. Even Fred Everett Maus's article on "Narratology, narrativity" for *The New Grove Dictionary of Music and Musicians* (2001) ends up in a rather doubtful position about the topic.

On the other hand, the interpretation of musical works as dramatic or plotted has achieved considerable success and currency. Four decades ago Charles Rosen (1971) articulated the compelling distinction between Baroque music and that of the Viennese Classics, identifying the earlier music-episteme as rhetoric while the latter depended on drama.[2] Anthony Newcomb (1984, 1987) has written about plot archetypes, particularly in the music of Schumann.[3] Maus (1988) offers some theory for music as drama. A 2008 book by Byron Almén, though titled *A Theory of Musical Narrative*, really develops in considerable detail the idea of musical plot.[4]

DEFINITION OF PLOT

Let us begin by examining the notion of plot in music. It makes sense to begin with Almén, since his book provides a recent and quite extensive discussion and has been widely read. He takes as his models some of the leading scholars in the fields of myth, semiotics, and fiction: James Jakób Liszka, Eero Tarasti, and Northrop Frye. In developing his theory, Almén offers several definitions of "narrative." Citing Liszka's *The Semiotic of Myth*, Almén presents a very technical definition:

> **Narrative** / A rule-like semiosis that revaluates the perceived, imagined, or conceived markedness and rank relations of a referent as delimited by the rank and markedness relations of the system of its

1. For a later resumption of the point, see Kivy (2009, 108–10).
2. As Rosen (1971, 43) puts it, "Dramatic sentiment was replaced by dramatic action."
3. For his application to an interpretation of Mahler, see also Newcomb (1992).
4. See the author's review of Almén's study in *Journal of Musicological Research* (Seaton 2011).

> signans and the teleology of the sign user (Liszka 1989:71). (Almén 2008, 224)

But Almén can also give less jargon-laden and clearer statements:

> . . . narrative involves the coordination of multiple elements: the articulation of conflicting elements or possibilities, their temporal engagement resulting in shifts of hierarchical emphasis, and an interpretive frame that establishes a meaningful perspective of the whole. (9)

> I will understand narrative as articulating the dynamics and possible outcomes of conflict or interaction between elements, rendering meaningful the temporal succession of events, and coordinating these events into an interpretive whole. (13)

I can fully subscribe to these descriptions, except that I do not believe that they are definitions of *narrative* but rather of *plot*, or of myth. With that important caveat—and with the promise that we shall return later to a more precise application of the concept of narrative, at an appropriate place in our discussion—I think that we can proceed in harmony.

In the latter half of his study Almén manages a sophisticated application of Frye's typology of plots, according to which we can classify stories as romance, tragedy, irony, and comedy. For his examples he draws in one instance on Susan McClary's work, but largely on analyses of Mahler symphonies and the writing of Vera Micznik (and indeed Almén's own work has focused on Mahler). In the case of Mahler in particular, the works themselves date from so much later than the conventional models of their genre that we can easily identify the transgressions against existing norms that allow us to classify the music according to Frye's four categories. In fact, Almén even finds it possible to locate certain works according to the phases within the ironic plot model. In doing so, he hears the symphonies as engaging cultural values.

While Almén's work constitutes a thought-provoking approach to the problem of plot in music, I intend something perhaps more modest. For one thing, my application of the concept of plot operates simply in regard to music itself, and when I apply cultural interpretation, it remains at a deeper, more abstract level than Almén's. The definition that I shall develop here focuses on fundamental principles in order to support a demonstration of how early-nineteenth-century music can be understood in terms of contemporaneous artistic premises.

As I have argued elsewhere (Seaton 2010), the history of music unfolds most essentially as the development of changing models for musical expression, grounded in what Michel Foucault (1971) would identify as the governing epistemes of contemporary culture and thought. As I outline these, thinkers before the fifteenth century conceived music as expressing divine and natural truth through number, using mathematical and harmonic principles. As Humanism took hold, the earlier episteme gave way to a new one, which produced music understood as relying on verbal expression, mimesis, and poetry. The period of Rationalism turned away from poetry for its model for musical expression and toward rhetoric as the means by which to express and move the passions or affections.

Coming to the Enlightenment, then, the episteme shifted again, and, as Rosen argued over four decades ago, the model for expression turned from rhetoric to drama. Here the construction and understanding of music as plotted properly takes hold. As Romanticism grew from the Enlightenment, it did not fundamentally abandon plot as music's expressive means. Having quickly arrived at the early nineteenth century, where our discussion will remain, for the moment let us pause there to consider what plot is, and then we shall explore how it manifests itself in some of Mendelssohn's music.

Let me begin by asserting, in cordial agreement with Almén, that to identify plot in music must not mean that we regard the music as merely derivative of literature. To the contrary, the idea of plot—thinking or perceiving any work in plotted terms—stands as a fundamental, epistemological concept. It might manifest itself in a verbal medium and in staged action, as it does in a play. Equally, it could govern a series of paintings, such as Hogarth's *The Rake's Progress*. So it should not seem difficult to understand that when a musical work has a plot, it can unfold that plot in exclusively musical terms. This explains the irrelevance of Nattiez's worries about the inability of a musical work to specify what it is "about." The work—at least in music of the Enlightenment—enacts itself.

In fact, the same holds true for a stage play. Shakespeare's *A Midsummer Night's Dream* does not represent actions that have taken place in the real world. In watching the play, we do not attempt to interpret it as reportage of actual people and events. The Aristotelian concept of mimesis, often articulated in the statement that artistic creation imitates humans in action, does not mean that art depicts particular people performing particular acts. As Aristotle puts it, "it is the function of a poet to relate not things that have happened, but things that may happen" (Aristotle 1987, 12). The work of art represents intentional actions, not actual ones, and this applies to music as well as to the theatre.

Whether in literature, dance and pantomime, visual art, or music, therefore, plot as a concept operates in transmedial ways. It will manifest the same attributes wherever we encounter it, so plot can be defined as experience in which we perceive these attributes. They include the following:

1. *Articulated and identifiable events.* Although this might seem self-evident, we should not overlook it. Of course, literary and stage drama contains events, and so do musical works. We might, of course, hear some pieces of early music as so brief or so static that they don't articulate themselves into events, in which case the work would not manifest plottedness. Visual art works more easily function without events—although some paintings certainly do represent or suggest events. On the other hand, a still life painting of a vase of flowers, for example, will not enact or portray a plot. We could also conceive a musical work so minimalist that no events occur in it, in which case it would not have a plot. Such conditions would not likely apply to music of the first half of the nineteenth century, of course.

2. *Characters/agents.* The presence and function of characters constitutes another essential component in a plot. A series of merely random or even of natural events does not satisfy our reasonable requirements of a plot (unless the forces of nature

are anthropomorphised in our imagination). Consequently, a literary plot more or less requires persons to accomplish this function, although the persons may be represented as gods or animals. We recognise them by their character qualities—for example, masculine or feminine; outgoing or introverted; self-possessed or flighty—and we expect certain characters to act in certain ways. They need not do so, of course, and when they do not, that contradiction of conventional expectation carries its own interest.

Within the usual framework of musical plots the functions of characters/agents typically belong to musical themes, largely as a function of rhythmic/melodic identity but also affected by scoring, dynamics, harmonic style, and texture. As a matter of fact, what we have become accustomed to calling by the rhetorical term *topos*, following the usage of Leonard Ratner (1980) in regard to eighteenth-century music, writers of the Enlightenment and early Romantic period commonly called *character*. I promise to provide at least one quotation to serve as a model example of a critic describing a musical theme explicitly in terms of its character.

The agency of musical themes might seem a bit more difficult to establish than their character, but I would argue that themes do perform functions and make things happen within a musical movement or piece. They certainly enter and depart, they introduce passages, they establish keys or lead from one key to another, they inter-*act* in alternation or in counterpoint.

3. *Situation.* We expect a plot to start from somewhere. This could include both a place and a set of circumstances. If we arrive at the theatre in the middle of a performance, we might see many events and learn to know the characters, but we would not properly say that we have experienced the plot. From the point of view of musical works in the idiom that we have before us now, the initial situation most generally consists of the key established at the start of the piece.

4. *Rising tension.* An increase in tension also forms one of the central features of plot. The degree to which tension

increases may vary among different types of works; so, for example, a pastoral play brings less heightened tension than a heroic drama. In music we have the heroic and pastoral symphonies of Beethoven to illustrate this point. In the tonal language of the Enlightenment and Romantic periods, of course, rising tension comes from modulation—typically either to the dominant key or, in works that begin in minor keys, to the relative major.

5. *Conflict/complication.* The next stage of a plot consists of a period of conflict. This can include surprising events, threats to the integrity of the characters, continuing tension, and so on. In musical terms we would hear unexpected modulations, complexities of texture, fragmentation of themes, and the like.

6. *Resolution.* To resolve the plot the characters must meet some sort of fate and find themselves in a newly stable situation. To musicians one hardly needs to explain how a piece or movement achieves resolution, since we employ exactly this same term for the return to consonant harmony or to the tonic key that we would use in identifying the reestablishment of stability in any other kind of plot.

7. *Denouement.* Once the moment of resolution has arrived, it remains to sort out the consequences of the preceding action. A new situation obtains, the characters may emerge in some way changed, and they must find their places within the new setting (or fail to do so). Depending on what happens to the leading character (or protagonist), we identify a drama, or indeed any plot, as comedy or tragedy.

PLOT AND MUSICAL FORM

By this time it can hardly come as a surprise that this description of plot conforms exactly to the musical action that we conventionally call "sonata form." In 1969, two years before Charles Rosen articulated the new, dramatic essence of Enlightenment music, the philosopher Stanley Cavell observed that in the eighteenth century music became

> dramatic in a more fundamental sense . . . when it . . . achieved its own dramatic autonomy, worked out its progress in its own terms . . . [The dramatic nature of music in this period] is secured only with the establishment of tonality and has its climax in the development of sonata form . . . I will say that the quality we are to perceive is one of *directed motion*, controlled by relationships of keys, by rate of alternation, and by length and articulation of phrases. We do not know where this motion can stop and we do not understand why it has begun here, so we do not know where we stand nor why we are there. The drama consists in following this out and in finding out what it takes to follow this out. (Cavell [1969] 2002, 320–21)

To summarise in schematic form, I shall offer a diagrammatic representation, in a layout that I will continue to use as we engage with Mendelssohn's music. Table 1 shows the basic plan.[5]

---

5. The two leading recent studies of the form are Charles Rosen's *Sonata Forms* ([1980] 1988) and James Hepokoski and Warren Darcy's *Elements of Sonata Theory: Norms, Types, and Deformations in the Late-Eighteenth-Century Sonata* (2006). These studies have done much to expand our analytical vision and vocabulary. Both emphasise that movements whose unfolding manifests the practices generally gathered under the term "sonata form" employ those practices very diversely, and the authors describe and illustrate many of the possibilities. The fortunate result is that musicians these days learn not to think in terms of a single, "correct" blueprint for all sonata movements, thus avoiding the danger with what we all now dismiss as the "textbook" definition of the form. Hepokoski and Darcy notably use the term "deformation" for moments within a piece that depart from the "norm," and indeed deformations occur so normatively that since *Elements of Sonata Theory* appeared we hardly use the term "form" at all, opting (lest we appear naïve) to refer to what happens in every movement as a sonata deformation.

We might find even these detailed categorisations of identifiable sonata types, devices, and strategies troubling, however. Replacing the misleading idea of a single governing form with a rich catalogue of options vastly expands our analytical toolbox and adds precision to our vocabulary. It does not necessarily bring us to a direct experience of the always infinitely flexible ways in which individual musical works play with the possibilities of plot. As in the work of the Russian formalists in analysing folk tales—best exemplified in Vladimir Propp's *Morphology of the Folktale* (1968)—classification always reaches a limit short of entering into the particular story or musical work itself. I hasten to add that Rosen and Hepokoski and Darcy recognise this truth, as well.

Form division—Conventional designation	Plot contour	Harmonic level	Musical material	Typical thematic character
Introduction (optional)	Prologue	Leading to tonic	O: opening	Anticipatory
Part I—Exposition Section 1	Stable situation	Tonic	P: theme(s) associated with principal key	Affirmative, forceful
	Increasing tension	Modulatory	T: theme(s) associated with harmonic transition	Active
Section 2	Contrasting situation	Dominant (or relative major)	S: theme(s) associated with secondary key	Contrasting to P, often lyrical
			K: theme(s) associated with closing	Affirmative, often "stock" character
Part II Section 3—Development	Rising action to climax	Unstable	Development of previous material; new material (N) may be introduced	Unpredictable
Section 4—Reprise	Resolution and denouement	Arrival of tonic	P	As in exposition
		Tonic	(T), S, K	As in exposition, except that all characters are in stable position

Table 1. Sonata form as plot

A few comments about table 1. First, as the leftmost column shows, I always refer to the two parts and four sections of sonata form by numbers, in the manner of late-eighteenth-century theorists (for example, Kollmann 1799), rather than by the anachronistic terms "exposition," "development," and "recapitulation." I use the term "exposition," if at all, only in the sense in which we use it when discussing plots in literary contexts, and not as a musical term. Likewise, "development" refers to a process within a plot rather than a passage in a movement.[6]

Comparing the second column to the first shows how the parts and sections of a sonata form correspond to the phases of a plot. The third column then aligns harmonic functions with the contour of tension, conflict, and resolution in a plot. The two columns at the right lay out the conventional letter symbols for themes[7] and some typical characters that would be associated with their roles.

We must note briefly here that character and harmonic tension/resolution appear in movements other than those in sonata form, of course. We might want to identify movements that follow other plans as plotted, as well, but the same criteria would have to apply to those cases in principle.

My approach to the problem works in the opposite direction. I choose to outline the principles only in general terms, steering away from detailed analytical classifications. What will interest us here is the actual plot of each work, and we shall leave it to some other, more music-theoretical, examination to denominate features of the music in terms of type. We might call our present approach *idiographic*, in contrast to the *nomothetic* methodologies of Rosen and Hepokoski and Darcy (or of Propp). A groundbreaking study of diverse treatments of form, specifically classifying Mendelssohn's works, is Wingfield and Horton (2012).

6. Hepokoski and Darcy (2006) generally employ the term "space" for these passages (and in some contexts "zone"). Because music is temporal rather than spatial, however, the image risks imposing a misleading implication of static form rather than dramatic process in our thinking about how the music works. In fairness, we must note that sometimes, as in their overview in chapter 2, "Sonata Form as a Whole" (especially 14–20), they emphasise that the music of the eighteenth century embodies the concept of action (and momentarily they employ the term "action-space"), which indicates at the outset an inkling of the core principle of drama or plot that we might otherwise find neglected in the usage throughout *Elements of Sonata Theory*.

7. The letter abbreviations here were established by Jan LaRue in *Guidelines for Style Analysis* (1970). For a brief overview of sonata form showing the use of these sigla, see the second edition (LaRue 1992, 187–93).

A FIRST DEMONSTRATION: CHARACTER AND PLOT IN MENDELSSOHN'S PIANO QUARTET IN C MINOR, OP. 1, MOVEMENT 1

Now we can turn to Mendelssohn's music. We begin with the first movements of the three early piano quartets and the two mature trios. The first thing that we notice is that all these works are in minor keys, all modulate to the relative major for section 2, and in every case the S theme appears in the parallel major in section 4, although the movement ultimately closes in the tonic minor. To that extent, the five movements roughly share an underlying model. Nevertheless, these pieces differ from one another in profound ways. The characters of their themes vary remarkably, so that the relationships and developments that they experience lead to completely different events over the courses of the respective movements. Even more important, each arrives at its own sort of resolution and denouement.

The opening movement of the First Piano Quartet, composed in 1822, when the composer was just thirteen years old, unfolds as shown in table 2. The left half of this diagram shows the typical plot for a sonata form in C minor. The characters identified in the fifth column merit some consideration, however, in order to understand the events and the distinctive plot of this movement. The first theme (see figure 1), which I have described as gloomy (and Mendelssohn, to judge from his famous letter to Marc-André Souchay,[8] would quickly remind us that the music expresses feeling much more precisely in its own terms than words can ever do), derives much of its character from the emphasis on the minor sixth scale degree, appearing as $A\flat_3$ first in the viola in bar 2 and then the cello in bar 6, followed by $A\flat_4$ in the violin in bar 8. The $D\flat_5$ that appears three times in the piano in quick succession (bars 9, 11, 13) reinforces the effect.

8. See Souchay and Mendelssohn (1998, 1198–201).

Form division	Plot contour	Harmonic level	Musical material	Thematic character	Bar numbers
Part I	Stable situation	C minor	Px, Py, Pz in Vc, Va, Vn	Gloomy	1
Section 1	Increasing tension	Modulation	Begins with "retake" in Vc, Pno		32
Section 2	Contrasting situation	E♭ major	S in Vc, Va, Vn	Dolce, but flamboyant ("Io sono docile"!)	56
			Px, Px^{i}, Py, K	Aggressive	90
Part II	Rising action	Unstable: e♭, e, d,	Development of Px, Px^{i},		106
Section 3	to climax	→ V/c	Py, Pz, K, (S?); ends with Eingang		
Section 4	Resolution and denouement	Arrival of C minor	Px, Py, Pz in Vc, Va, Vn	Gloomy	191
		C major	S in Pno, Vn	Dolce, but flamboyant	230
			Px, Px^{i}, Py, K	Aggressive	268
Coda		C minor	cpt. → Px^{dim}	Learned → Extroverted	286–300

P – Modelled on Mozart; S – Quotation from Rossini

Table 2. Form of Mendelssohn, Piano Quartet in C minor, op. 1 (MWV Q11), movement 1

Figure 1. Piano Quartet in C minor, op. 1 (MWV Q11), movement 1, bars 1–9

Also noteworthy, the theme has a complex design, consisting of three contrasting elements, which unfold across the three string instruments in succession—the surging triadic outline in the cello (Px); the attempted continuation of that rising gesture in the viola, which soon wilts into a chromatic descent and then settles on scale degree $\hat{5}$ (Py); and the nearly paralysed conclusion of repeated notes in the violin, able to manage hardly any more activity than the step up a minor second before slipping back again (Pz).

The first reviews of this work, in the Leipzig *Allgemeine musikalische Zeitung* and the *Berliner allgemeine musikalische Zeitung*, observed that it suggested Mozart as its model, although more in the working out than in specific reminiscences.[9] We might note, though, that Mozart's music does offer some models for gloomy themes in C minor. The Piano Concerto KV 491, for example, opens with a unison theme that rises from C through E♭ to A♭ and then slips back through G to F♯. The so-called "Dissonance" String Quartet, KV 465, begins with a throbbing C in the cello, above which the viola enters on A♭ and descends via G to F♯, while the second violin introduces E♭.[10]

If the character of P brings to mind predecessors of its type in the works of Mozart, then that of theme S (bars 56–62) makes a reference so unmistakable as to seem amusing (see figure 2). The setting here evokes an operatic aria in its elementary accompaniment for the piano, over which the cello melody clearly alludes to Rosina's first-act aria in *Il barbiere di Siviglia*, "Una voce poco fa," at the line "Io sono docile." The expression marking is *dolce*. The piano supports the continuation of the moment, as first the viola and then the violin respond with their own melismatic flamboyance.

9. In the *Allgemeine musikalische Zeitung* J. P. Schmidt (1824, 184) wrote, "Mozart bleibe stets das Vorbild des, sich mit eigener Geisteskraft entwickelnden Talents, bis zur Erreichung des weit gesteckten Zieles." Meanwhile, in the *Berliner allgemeine musikalische Zeitung*, an anonymous reviewer, probably Ludwig Rellstab, wrote: "Um kurz zu sein, wollen wir nur im Allgemeinen bemerken, dass sich der Komponist Mozart zum vorbilde gewählt hat. R. sucht die Wahrheit seiner Bemerkung nicht in einem Haschen nach etwanigen Reminiscenzen aus Mozart zu unterstützen, sondern er findet das im Wesentlichen in dem, was man Arbeit nennt, bestätigt" ([Rellstab?] 1824, 168).

10. R. Larry Todd (2003, 105) points out the resemblance of the thematic treatment here—the rising C-minor arpeggio answered by the rising dominant arpeggio—to the opening of Mozart's Piano Sonata in C minor, KV 457.

Figure 2. Piano Quartet in C minor, op. 1 (MWV Q11), movement 1, bars 56–66

As the movement's plot restabilises in E♭ (bars 90–105), the P theme begins to re-emerge in this new environment, asserting control over the situation. In this context it adopts the guise of forcefulness and energy, not only in the major key but also fortissimo. It adds a triadic descent in contrary motion against the initial rise, and it loses its static concluding element. Alternating with the components of P, a new closing thematic element, K (bars 94–98), supports this plot event.

The plot development that begins at the end of section 2 continues into the conflict and instability of section 3. The characteristic features of P all come into play, but nothing of S, although fourteen bars of eighth-note motion in the piano might suggest a reminiscence of its flair (bars 138–51). The energy dissipates as little more than the unenergetic Pz motive remains, along with the collapsing inversion of Px. But a crescendo leads to an ad libitum *Eingang* flourish from the piano (bar 190) and a pause on the unresolved dominant.

The resolution comes as the character of P reasserts itself, intact, in C minor. Theme S follows (bars 230–44), bringing with it the major key, altered in its scoring to begin now with the piano accompanied by the strings, abbreviated by the omission of the uninteresting part formerly assigned to the viola. The mood shifts back to minor as two bars of dominant seventh from the piano lead to two more of the dominant ninth chord with A♭, and the version of P that closed off Part 1 returns again in C minor (bars 264–78). A fifteen-bar coda (bars 286–300) concludes the movement, notably featuring three rapid, fortissimo statements of the rising triadic motive in rhythmic diminution.

Looking back at character and plot in the first movement of op. 1, we might summarise by observing that the two themes act in roles for which each seems distinctively suited. S, which possesses a superficially lively but empty character, does not really participate in significant action. It does not even develop to the extent of recognising the overall minor shading of the situation at the denouement; at most, it appears to have dressed itself slightly differently than at first and shed its least interesting feature. P, by contrast, in its complexity and flexibility, engages insistently in any context and action, occupying the plot wherever substantive development occurs.

Can we find in this early and modest piece some significant meaning, along the lines that Susan McClary, Lawrence Kramer, or Byron Almén might draw out of a more imposing work? I would not want to strain too hard in this direction. Yet one could, at least, hear such a plot as a model, demonstrating abstract character qualities and their potentialities, an axiomatic statement about art or life. The particular intertextual references that attach to the two main themes' characters, however, open up the possibility to hear the movement as a critique of the character of the post-revolutionary Restoration, revealed as naïve, while the values of the Enlightenment retain their strength and potentiality.

A SECOND DEMONSTRATION: THE PIANO QUARTET IN F MINOR, OP. 2, MOVEMENT I

Mendelssohn's Second Piano Quartet, composed a little more than one year later and dedicated to his composition teacher Karl Friedrich Zelter, proceeds in an entirely different way (see table 3).[11] What probably strikes the listener first is the character of the principal theme (see figure 3). Lyrical, symmetrical, and firmly closed after eight bars, it sings of sorrow, leaping first to the minor third and then to the minor sixth scale degree, each time falling back as the high pitch holds on for the duration of half a bar but then collapses stepwise in two quarter notes. The hearer should wonder whether such a lyrical theme can really function as agent in a complex plot.

A retake of P at bar 22 nearly forms a complete restatement of the static theme, but at the last moment it begins to reveal its potential for agency and development. The one-bar falling gesture detaches from the theme to launch the transition. At bar 58, as section 2 begins in A♭, that gesture marks the new territory. Then, as the passage proceeds, the introduction of the flat sixth scale degree (starting in bar 83), so prominently part of the character of P, begins to pervade the otherwise major-key environment. This flat sixth degree, framed by degree $\hat{5}$, makes unfulfilled yearning an inherent aspect of the heightened tension of the plot at this point.

11. *Dwight's Journal of Music* (1853, 118) on op. 2: "The Quartet by Mendelssohn, Op. 2, for Piano and strings, though one of his earliest works, in which the Mendelssohnian peculiarity is not very fully developed, . . ."

Form division	Plot contour	Harmonic level	Musical material	Thematic character	Bar numbers
Part I	Stable situation	f	P	Cantabile, sorrowful	1
Section 1	Increasing tension	Modulation	P (retake) and descending figure with free material	Cantabile, then virtuosic	22
Section 2	Contrasting situation	A♭	Derived from P	Simple, affirmative	58
			$\hat{5}$–♭$\hat{6}$–$\hat{5}$	Yearning	83ff
Part II Section 3	Rising action to climax	Unstable: D♭, b♭, F♯ (=G♭) → V/f	Development of P		128
Section 4	Resolution and denouement	Arrival of f	P	Cantabile, sorrowful then virtuosic	209
		F	Derived from P	Simple, affirmative	246
			$\hat{5}$–♭$\hat{6}$–$\hat{5}$	Yearning	
Coda		b♭ → f	Development of P	Tentative	314
			Stretta	Insistent	345–81

Table 3. Form of Mendelssohn, Piano Quartet in F minor, op. 2 (MWV Q13), movement 1

Figure 3. Piano Quartet in F minor, op. 2 (MWV Q13), movement 1, bars 1–8

The conflict played out in section 3, largely through the dark flat-side of the tonal spectrum, comes entirely to serve for the development of the opening leap and descent of P, a striving that tries to regain completeness in its variety of contexts. Yet none of these situations is sufficiently stable to allow it to establish itself securely. As it comes in sight of home—arriving at the governing dominant—it accelerates to double time and reaches fortissimo (bar 197), but then it only crashes onto the C-major chord. A chromatic scale from the piano, diminuendo, leads back to F minor (bar 209), where P regains its self-possession and recovers its lyric character.

The denouement starts to work out more or less as we would expect. Notably, in section 4 the recurrence of the $\hat{5}$ $\flat\hat{6}$ $\hat{5}$ figure within the F-major passage (starting in bar 279) reinforces the influence that the leading character has over whatever place it occupies. The coda opens with B♭ minor (bar 314), where we find P again seeking completeness but instead opening up into newly persistent development. This continues through the final *stretta* (bars 345–81), where the anacrusis now leaps from F to B♭ and descends back through the fourth to resolve on the tonic.

As we noted at the outset, this movement is superficially built on the same plot model as its predecessor, but it spins out an entirely different action. Almén (2008, 9) would probably identify this as an "introverted" plot, because it focuses on the development of a single, underlying motive. Here the leading character initially seems dubiously equipped for the course of a drama. As the tension rises and the new, contrasting situation is established, it demonstrates that aspects of its identity enable it for agency in these contexts. Having let go of its stable centre, it seeks destabilisation through dark regions and with increasing vigour until, having exhausted itself, it recuperates in its home position. Yet, having done this, the close of the denouement challenges it yet again, for its refragmentation threatens to undermine it once more—unless it were to retreat to its balanced, closed form. But, as it turns out, something else happens: it seizes on its strongest attribute, modifies that to a new purpose, and takes the opportunity to master the plot's conclusion.

This "introverted" plot holds considerable interest in its own right. It proposes a poised, if sorrowful, character, encountered as a fully formed identity, that nevertheless launches out on adventures that first present opportunities to apply itself in different situations and eventually challenge its ability to hold together. Having recovered itself, the character appears to have found how to employ its traits to gain control of its environment, but a final problem, that of bringing the plot to a decisive close, forces it to adapt one last time. At the conclusion, as in a sort of *Bildungs*-drama, though a purely musical one, mature self-development leads to a successful end.

Were we willing to indulge in a bit of fantasy and (auto)biographical fallacy, we might imagine the movement as representing the young composer's view toward his own future career—fully formed at the beginning, meeting conflict and growing, retaining his vital personality, and eventually finding in himself the means to shape his situation and his own end. But we should not go that route, and I suggest it here only in a rhetorically satirical sense.

Instead, I would like to reemphasise a crucial point. Hearing the plot of a musical movement does *not* mean paraphrasing the music into some sort of literary programme. My last bit of hypothetical biographical-fantasy programme aside, it should be clear that throughout my analytical descriptions I have treated the music in its own terms; nothing analytical in these descriptions should trouble even a hard-core formalist. To be sure, different critics might describe the character of a theme in different ways, or they might use different terms to express how the themes act within a movement.[12] Nevertheless, the themes do have character, they do have roles in the music, and pieces do play out plots. Hearing them in this way does not mean at all that we force some artificial, extramusical overlay onto them. To the contrary, we follow the music in a way not only musical but grounded in the Enlightenment and early Romantic episteme, and in the model for musical expression that emerged from it.

SOMETHING UNEXPECTED: THE PIANO QUARTET IN B MINOR, OP. 3, MOVEMENT I

About a year after op. 2 came op. 3, a third work in the same genre. Its first movement presents yet another plot, and this one takes a considerably more unusual twist (see table 4).

12. This is, of course, precisely the point made by Mendelssohn himself in his letter to Marc-André Souchay (see Souchay and Mendelssohn 1998).

Form division	Plot contour	Harmonic level	Musical material	Thematic character	Bar numbers
Part I	Stable situation	b	P (beginning with motive p, includes two extensions: 1X, 2X)	Intense, introverted; courtly	1
Section 1	Increasing tension	Modulation			
Section 2	Contrasting situation	D	2X + p	Convivial	110
Part II	Rising action to climax	C	N	Striving	247
Section 3		g, a, b, e♭, d, b	N + p	+ intense	
Section 4	Resolution and denouement	Arrival of b	P	Intense, introverted; courtly	393
		B	2X + p	Convivial	436
Coda		b–C–b	N	Striving—and fulfilled	560–628

Table 4. Form of Mendelssohn, Piano Quartet in B minor, op. 3 (MWV Q17), movement 1

In some ways, the thematic generation of the first part somewhat resembles that of the movement that we have just discussed. Here the main theme (see figure 4) opens with another kind of lyrical line, beginning in this case with a constricted, chromatic turn around the first degree of the scale, then climbing through an octave and quickly falling all the way back to the leading tone (bars 1–8).

Figure 4. Piano Quartet in B minor, op. 3 (MWV Q17), movement 1, bars 1–24

Here, as promised, comes the opportunity to observe how the period thought of themes and expressed them in terms of character. Ludwig Rellstab reviewed the Third Piano Quartet, describing this music as follows:

> The character of the theme, as of the whole movement, is a feeling stirred up by unease, but which knows how to keep itself within its limits and, as it approaches passion, yields itself again to its secret dissatisfaction. The first two bars form the main motive of the movement. The second bar's minor ninth gives a glimpse of melancholy, which emerges admirably in the strings. The cello has to play the low notes in this passage especially *pesante.* The clothing of the main passagework in triplets should on the one hand be described as *natural,* and the tempo and pace extremely measured. (Rellstab 1825, 354, my translation)[13]

13. "Der Karakter des Themas, so wie des ganzen Satzes, ist ein durch Unruhe aufgeregtes Gefühl, welches sich aber in seinen Schranken zu halten weiss und, so wie es sich der Leidenschaft nähert, sich auch wieder seinem geheimen Unmuth überlässt. Die Hauptfigur des Satzes bilden die ersten beiden Takte. Die kleine None des zweiten Taktes giebt einen Schwermuthsblick, der sich in den Streichinstrumenten vortrefflich hervorthut. Besonders *pesant* hat das Cello in den tiefen Tönen diese Stelle zu spielen. Die Einkleidung der Hauptpassagen in Triolen ist auf der einen Seite allerdings *natürlich* zu nennen, und dem Tempo und Zeitmaass äusserst angemessen."

After four bars that move to the subdominant (bars 9–13), an extension (bars 10–20) brings the music around to a cadence on the tonic in a style that evokes the courtly eighteenth century. A second extension, apparently a rather simple-minded and repetitious cadential formula, follows (bars 25–47). A retake of P (starting in bar 48) initiates the rise of tension.

In a plot move not entirely different from that in the corresponding movement in op. 2, the material that establishes the area of contrast, D major, derives from part of P. In fact, the second extension now comes into its true character, for the texture and range allude to the Männerchor, and in the major mode the spirit is one of conviviality (bars 110–16). Nevertheless, the section also features numerous appearances of the intense, introverted, turning figure of P.

We should note here that, for the first time, part 1 does not conclude with a repeat sign but continues directly into section 3. After the cadence in D in bar 227 comes a slow, mysterious transition that leads to the dominant of C. The plot twist occurs at the start of section 3 (bar 247), where an entirely new character enters in C major (theme N; see figure 5). It presses upward, striving through the sharp-fourth scale degree to reach the fifth. This character engages with the inward-turning P motive through a long series of minor-key centres.

Theme/character N eventually gives way as the tonic approaches, so that P can return in B minor, as it does, essentially intact as at the beginning (bar 393). The conviviality of section 2 comes very easily (bar 440), to set up a long passage in B major, full of considerable energy but lacking notable thematic character. After a brief allusion to the hushed music that led to section 3, but now with no modulation, the denouement stalls on a dominant chord (bar 559).

A final surprise awaits. At the coda the principal character has entirely departed. Instead, the striving theme N re-enters in B minor (bar 560). It ultimately presses upward all the way through A sharp to the upper octave B (bar 616), achieving fulfilment and accomplishing the final resolution of its own plot.

Figure 5. Piano Quartet in B minor, op. 3 (MWV Q17), movement 1, bars 247–57

This imaginative plot presents two interlocking developments. One traces the rather multifaceted character of P through a generally standard sort of contour. The other begins when a completely foreign character, N in C major, disrupts that contour at the start of section 3 and resolves only after P's denouement, ultimately assimilating N to B minor, where it reaches its fulfilment.

MATURITY AND EXPERIMENT: THE PIANO TRIO NO. 1 IN D MINOR, OP. 49 (MWV Q29), MOVEMENT 1

In the two great piano trios, works of his maturity, Mendelssohn worked out his plots in a way that departs quite strikingly from the Classic sonata form model.[14] The first of these, the Piano Trio in D minor, op. 49, dates from 1839. Its opening movement represents the change clearly. Like the Third Piano Quartet, this movement eschews the repetition of part 1 (which would, of course, make Kivy less sceptical about narrativity in these cases), but whereas in the earlier piece this did not directly affect the ensuing progress of the plot, the Trio's plot draws important consequences from this feature.

The first three sections of the movement lay out a plot that unfolds in an interesting but not radically unusual manner. As table 5 shows, the plot stretches out at the end, however, so that although the harmonic resolution arrives as expected in bar 368, almost half the movement remains. This explores new possibilities for the development of the themes' characters. At bar 368 the cello's character from the opening returns, this time with the added complexity of an enriching counterpoint from the violin. The secondary theme follows quite soon, not much changed from at first, and a more strained version of the principal theme, already heard at bar 187, comes again at bar 503.

14. Klaus Wolfgang Niemöller (2004) provides a thoughtful consideration of the two Piano Trios, relying on the terms "Charakter" and "Dramaturgie," although without any extensive definition of those concepts.

Form division	Plot contour	Harmonic level	Musical material	Thematic character	Bar numbers
Part I	Stable situation	d	P	Sombre, agitated	1
Section 1	Increasing tension	Modulation	P retake and free material	Now stern	
Section 2	Contrasting situation	A	S	Peaceful, stable	119
		→	K	Agitated	163
		a	P	Now strained	187
Part II	Rising action to climax	Unstable: a, g	Development of P		222
Section 3		B♭, g, c, C, A	S (P fragments)		
Section 4	Resolution and denouement	Arrival of d	P	Sombre, agitated; added layer of complexity	368
		D	S	Peaceful, stable	435
		→	K	Agitated	478
		d	P	Strained	503
Coda		d	P	Desperate	540
		D	S	Triumphant	558
		D	P	Insistent	604–16

Table 5. Form of Mendelssohn, Piano Trio in D minor, op. 49, movement 1

The coda brings more striking character developments. At bar 540 a new version of P enters fortissimo, with a sense of desperation, in imitation between violin and cello. S re-enters, also fortissimo, so that whereas we had previously encountered it as secure and stable, pianissimo and espressivo at bar 119 or piano and dolce at bar 435, now it strides out triumphantly (bar 558). One final brief and desperate appearance of P, fortissimo and in octaves in the strings, is cut off by four cadential hammer blows.

We might describe this plot as exploring the self-determined fates of the two main contrasting characters. The figure introduced at the opening as both sombre and agitated proceeds through conflict to regain stability, but it seems dissatisfied with stability and demands to change and intensify until its only possible ending, a ruthless and abrupt one. Meanwhile the peaceful and stable character of S allows it to become triumphant, retaining its major-key optimism but ending in a position of strength. Given the nineteenth-century inclination toward or recognition of the gendered characters of themes in sonata-plot works, we could say that the normatively masculine P theme demonstrates a masculine course of development and a determined (or overdetermined) but catastrophic ending, while the normatively feminised S theme attains heroic fulfilment.

EXTENDED CHARACTER DEVELOPMENT IN SECTION 4 REVISITED: THE PIANO TRIO NO. 2 IN C MINOR, OP. 66 (MWV Q33), MOVEMENT I

Something rather similar takes place in the first movement of the Second Piano Trio (see table 6). Again the characters enter in ways that we might well expect (figure 6), and the action follows conventional plot lines through the establishment of a stable point of origin, a rise of tension, and complication and conflict. As with the Piano Trio no. 1, at the denouement the P theme returns (bar 220) with the revelation of a previously unknown potentiality, here not merely with a counter-element but as a canon (see figure 7), thus much more organically and intellectually developed. The S theme enters less solidly than at its first appearance.

Figure 6. Piano Trio in C minor, op. 66 (MWV Q33), movement 1, bars 1–10

Figure 7. Piano Trio in C minor, op. 66 (MWV Q33), movement 1, bars 221–26

As the denouement proceeds, we encounter more harmonic surprise and more developmental texture than in the equivalent late phases of the earlier trio. A long, anticipatory passage (bars 293–352) leads up to the re-entry of P (bar 353), now complicated by its simultaneous presentation by the piano as at first and by the violin in augmentation (see figure 8)—again a somewhat organic and intellectual amplification of the character. Toward the end S re-emerges in F minor (bar 385), at first in a stressful state but quickly becoming reflective, hesitating, and stopping on a dominant seventh. P steps in forcefully to lead from F minor rapidly back to C minor for the close (bars 393–99).

Form division	Plot contour	Harmonic level	Musical material	Thematic character	Bar numbers
Part I	Stable situation	c	1P	Constrained energy	1
Section 1			2P	Moody	23
	Increasing tension		1P retake	Constrained energy	42
Section 2	Contrasting situation	E♭	S	Grounded, strong; then quietly secure	63, 79
Part II	Rising action to	Unstable: g, . . .	Development of 1P, 2P		95
Section 3	climax	D♭	S		156
Section 4	Resolution and denouement	Arrival of c	1P (canonic)	Constrained energy with new potentiality revealed	221
		C	S	Quietly secure	242, 258
		C	2P	Moody	271
		C: V → f: V → C: ♭VI → V	Development of 1P		293
Coda		C	1P (with augmentation)	New potentiality revealed	353
		f	S	Stressed, then reflective	385
		f→c	1P	Forceful	393

Table 6. Form of Mendelssohn, Piano Trio in C minor, op. 66 (MWV Q33), movement 1

Figure 8. Piano Trio in C minor, op. 66 (MWV Q33), movement 1, bars 353–56

This opening movement of the C-minor Trio, like its parallel in the D-minor Trio, also drops the repetition of the first part and balances that by an extended and developmental denouement. The character development and working-out of the plot takes quite a different turn, however. The S theme, perhaps also a feminine-gendered one, arrives at the end not at triumph but confusion. The P theme does not so much play out masculine impulses as explore a kind of intellectual self-development. At the very close we do not hear the P theme sharply cut off by loud blows; instead, the confusion of S's F minor is cleared up by the forceful triadic intervention of P.

SUMMARY: CHARACTER AND PLOT

To conclude up to this point, this demonstration of these diverse movements shows the potentiality of a plot analysis for instrumental movements in sonata form. (The principles can also be applied, of course, though not quite so straightforwardly, to tonal works in other forms.) The treatment of these movements has relied on two basic premises, which we hold at the forefront of our attention as we hear the music.

The first premise: in music of the Enlightenment and Romanticism, themes have character. As we have noted, when we read the writings of theorists of the period, we find that they use "character" as the most common way of referring to the expressive nature of musical ideas. We have long recognised this in what we have called "topic" analysis. In the eighteenth century, themes adopted conventional characters: military, courtly, rustic, ecclesiastical, and so on. Approaching Romanticism, composers found more individual kinds of themes, a trend that of course reflects the essence of Romanticism itself. As a result, we have to identify character through emotional terms, often more complexly than single words can manage. One important distinction that the period itself made, specifically in relation to themes in sonata form, viewed character as intrinsically gendered. To be sure, different listeners might describe a musical character in different words; Mendelssohn would hasten to remind us, however, that the character of the music remains always clear and precise and that only the words we use are ambiguous.

The second premise: tonally conceived musical forms produce contours of stability, tension, conflict, and resolution. In fact, this really amounts to a tautology. It means that the potential for plot exists in all tonal music. That potential reached its model manifestation in sonata plots, in which the prolongation of tonic, dominant, and return to the tonic govern the entire length of a movement. We should not forget that Mozart in his operas instantiated the dramatic opportunities of tonality by employing sonata-like harmonic plans to carry his characters (i.e., musical qualities) and personages (i.e., human dramatis personae) through the action in setting operatic ensembles.

And so, because the music of the eighteenth and nineteenth centuries intentionally expresses characters and adopts dramatic contour, a theory of plot offers our best explanatory and interpretive tool for dealing with the forms of musical movements in this period and style.

A NOTE ON ARCHETYPE AND MYTH: MEANINGS IN PLOTS

Since so much of the literature on music and plot relies on the relationships of plot, archetype, and myth, these deserve a brief comment at this point. We must frame our observations, however, by reemphasising the caveat that music does not report something other than music. In all this discussion so far I have only observed what actually happens in the music itself, never suggesting that a movement illustrates something else that we understand to have taken place in the real or a literary world.

More generally, to reveal a plot as an instance of an archetype is valuable, if we resist any inclination to think that the music is *about* some other—literary—instance of the archetype.[15] In fact, taken broadly, sonata form amounts to an archetype for plots generally, whether musical or literary ones. The development of this archetype arose in the eighteenth century as a manifestation of Enlightenment epistemology, just as, and simultaneously with, the English novel.

We might then think of a myth as a story that unfolds an epistemologically based archetype in such a way that it enacts and expresses the values of a culture. The critic can therefore reasonably interpret a plot—whether retold in oral myth, acted on the stage, read from the page, or heard in music—to learn some core truth espoused by the culture from which that plot came.

15. Thus, if we observe that a Brahms intermezzo and a short story by Henry James share some central features of plot, we must not understand Brahms's piano piece as recounting James's story (see Jordan and Kafalenos 1989). The conclusion here is quite correct: the parallelism between the two indicates that they both share predispositions inherent in late-nineteenth-century thinking.

DEFINITION OF NARRATIVE

So far we have dealt with plot, but I have resisted any inclination to employ the term "narrative." Let us move now to that somewhat more challenging problem. The first task consists of defining and explaining what we should best mean by narrative. Then we will outline some of the means by which we can identify narrativity in music. To make the method concrete, we can illustrate by applying representative methods to these Mendelssohn works of chamber music with piano—despite the fact that, as I have said previously, these works constitute an admittedly unlikely repertoire for such a project.

A simple, clear, and, to my way of thinking, compelling definition of the concept appears in a 1966 study by Robert Scholes and Robert Kellogg, *The Nature of Narrative* (4). They wrote, "By narrative we mean all those literary works which are distinguished by two characteristics: the presence of a story and a story-teller. A drama is a story without a story-teller; . . . . For writing to be narrative no more and no less than a teller and a tale are required." In a narrative, then, the action forms the plot and the narrator forms the voice, the subjectivity, the persona behind the story.

As we have seen, a large-scale first movement in Enlightenment or Romantic instrumental music depends on a plotted model for expression. Plot alone does not make a narrative, however. It merely makes drama. Our descriptions of the movements that we have discussed so far have treated them as dramas, not as narratives. When we watch a play by, for example, Sophocles or Shakespeare or Racine, we generally do not find our attention drawn from the action to an awareness of a storyteller. We tend to focus on the characters and the events in the plot, so that we do not, in fact, look for the voice of someone telling the story of *Antigone*, or *A Midsummer Night's Dream*, or *Athalie*. In this context, we experience the work as drama but not narrative—at least not narrative in what I would call the "strong" sense of the term, and I shall force myself to hold to that "strong" definition.

My thinking here owes much to my reading of Mikhail Bakhtin. In his essays published in English translation as

The Dialogic Imagination (1981) he asserts that a fundamental aspect of narrative is the distinction between two interlocking levels—the story and the frame—and these generally maintain their respective identities through their manners of discourse (though, of course, they can also become entangled). Robert Hatten has also written about levels of discourse in his work on Beethoven (see Hatten 1991). Other influences on my thinking include Edward Cone, whose book *The Composer's Voice* (1974) holds a seminal place in musical narratology, and Lawrence Kramer, who helpfully describes other-voicedness in his chapter on the uncanny in *Music as Cultural Practice, 1800–1900* (1990). As part of our task, we should attend to shifts of level, juxtapositions of idioms or intonations, and disruption in the discourse of the music that we study, hearing in these the indications of narrative voice.

NARRATIVE PERSONA AND ROMANTICISM

Additionally, I find myself interested in the degree to which we can identify or actually give a fictive name to the narrative voice, when we can discern this within a piece of music. As well as the word "voice" in his book's title, Cone uses the term "persona." Others—Dahlhaus, for example—might refer to the work's "aesthetic subject."[16] Because the word "subject" has so many potential meanings in music, ranging from the melodic unit that serves as the basis for a fugue, to the object depicted by a characteristic piece, as well as referring to a narrative voice, it becomes a bit problematic. With my students I have tended to refer to this as the "individual subjectivity." Now the presence of such a subjectivity behind a musical work has seemed to me the most compelling rationale for classifying that work as Romantic. In fact, I have leaned of late toward separating music of the nineteenth century into separate categories for genuinely Romantic works (those that manifest an underlying individual

16. A clear and useful discussion of the principle may be found in the introductory chapter in Dahlhaus's *Ludwig van Beethoven: Approaches to His Music* (1991, 1–42).

subjectivity) and what I would call post-Classic or post-Enlightenment works. The Romantic is perceived wherever a narrative voice, a fictive persona, emerges in the experience of a work.

LOCATING THE NARRATIVE VOICE: METHODOLOGY

We must turn now to the problem of locating the narrative voice. To begin with, we have to clear up one common source of confusion. The question most often asked, and the one that tripped up, for example, Nattiez, has to do with the notion that the music narrates some sort of extramusical story. As we have established, however, music *enacts* plot, it does not recount plot. This is why the question that Carolyn Abbate (1989, 222) suggests, "How does music narrate?," leads us in a fruitless direction. Musical narratology should instead ask *who narrates music*. The narrative voice stands behind the musical plot. We should expect only rarely to hear that voice explicitly. Instead, we locate and identify it by other means. Some of these emerge from the music as we hear it, but we can encounter other indications, as well.

EXTRAMUSICAL OR PARATEXTUAL INDICATIONS OF VOICE

We might begin by noting that the identification of an individual subjectivity behind music became an essential concern of nineteenth-century listeners and critics; far from an idea imposed by recent critical theory, this represented a vital aspect of nineteenth-century understanding. This explains the burst of interest in composers' biographies beginning around 1800. Readers believed that knowledge of the composer as an individual would provide insight into the music itself. (This can lead, of course, to two less desirable results. On one hand, it promotes the biographical fallacy, whereby the listener or critic interprets a work as merely the composer's autobiography. On the other, it leads to the cultivation of romanticised biography writing, artificially imposing on the composer's actual life the expressive content of the music.)

An obvious instance of the construction of musical personas comes from the writings of Robert Schumann. From his first published review of Chopin we meet Florestan and Eusebius and their companions, and in the *Davidsbündlertänze*, op. 6, individual movements bore the initials F. or E.—or both. Of course, Schumann also created a persona for Mendelssohn under the name "F. Meritis." By the time of the Piano Trios, Schumann had given up the device of the Davidsbündler, but even so he frames his review of the D-minor Trio, op. 49, by assigning a sort of persona,

> . . . the child of his epoch. He also had to struggle; also had to listen to the nonsensical jabber of the narrow-minded: "The real springtime of music lies behind us"; and he has raised himself so high that we can indeed say he is the Mozart of the nineteenth century; the most brilliant among musicians; the one who has most clearly recognized the contradictions of the time, and the first to reconcile them. (Schumann 1946, 217)[17]

Schumann's portrayal of course represents a statement about the *composer*, but it also invokes a certain narrative *persona*, inviting his reader to hear the Trio's plot as a statement in a contemporary voice, brilliantly musical by comparison even with Mozart, the model composer who represented natural and boundless genius, and also a penetrating mind, specifically taking up and resolving the essential and inherent problems of his era.

In many cases nineteenth-century composers themselves provided paratextual material that locates and identifies the music's individual subjectivity. To cite one of my favourite examples, Liszt's "Vallée d'Obermann" not only identifies its persona by association with Senancour's novel and has as a prefatory note excerpted statements by the title character, but it also bears an additional quotation from Byron's Childe Harold. Further, the listener must understand the music in terms created by the titles of the collections in which it appeared—at one time as the experience of a traveller, in the *Album d'un voyageur*, and at another as that of a pilgrim, in the *Années de pèlerinage*.

17. It is worth noting here that in his review of Chopin's op. 2 Schumann had already set up Mozart as a fictive composer for the variations on "Là ci darem la mano."

We certainly do not find that sort of paratextual assistance in Mendelssohn's chamber music. Yet an interesting source by which to approach the voice of the music exists in the form of the dedications of these works, of which one in particular I find striking. Especially in a historical context in which, unlike in the eighteenth century, the work does not primarily serve to glorify a patron, a dedication might identify a narratee addressed by the music and consequently imply a certain narrator. Here is a list of the dedicatees of Mendelssohn's chamber music with piano (for those works that bore dedications), including the works that we have not discussed in detail:

- Piano Quartet in C minor, op. 1—Prince Antoni Henryk Radziwiłł (1775–1833), cellist and composer
- Piano Quartet in F minor, op. 2—Carl Friedrich Zelter (1758–1832), composer and Mendelssohn's teacher
- Piano Quartet in B minor, op. 3—Johann Wolfgang von Goethe (1749–1832), poet (etc.)
- Violin Sonata in F minor, op. 4—Eduard Rietz (1802–32), violinist and Mendelssohn's friend
- Variations concertantes for cello and piano, op. 17—Paul Mendelssohn Bartholdy (1812–74), Mendelssohn's brother, amateur cellist
- Cello Sonata no. 2 in D major, op. 58—Count Mateusz Wielhorski (1794–1866), cellist and patron
- Piano Trio in C minor, op. 66—Louis Spohr (1784–1859), violinist and composer
- Lied ohne Worte for cello and piano, op. 109—Lisa Cristiani (1827–53), cellist

One dedication seems particularly intriguing, for it addresses a non-musician. Zelter had introduced his twelve-year-old protégé to his friend Goethe in Weimar in 1821, and the aging poet and eager young boy had become friends. At sixteen Mendelssohn made Goethe the narratee of the B-minor Quartet. We can easily imagine a number of qualities that this then implies for the narrative voice, as well—association with elite social and intellectual circles, personal affection rather than professional colleagueship or practicality, an inclination toward the poetic or other disciplines generally. All these certainly apply to the composer as well as to the voice in the work.

Yet another line of thinking opens itself here if we consider the dedication in relation to the plot of the B-minor Trio's first movement, which we have already studied. As we have seen, the P theme extends through a rather intense character at the opening, extended to a courtly aspect and then to an image of sociable conviviality. The remarkable feature of the plot is the intrusion of the unanticipated character N, with its rising aspirations, at the beginning of the plot's complication. After the completion of the denouement for the main characters, N takes the stage and achieves its own maturity and fulfilment. Could Goethe have followed this plot? Did Mendelssohn expect him to do so? Whatever the case, we should not overlook that the aspiring, youthful composer addressed the great man with a plot that surely suggests a kind of musical *Bildung*-experience for a latecomer, set against an intellectual, courtly, and convivial backdrop—a sort of invented, purely musical (and, I hasten to emphasise, purely fictive), Weimar.

To be sure, the dedications can provide a far less complicated sort of case for a voice. The clear example of the Cello Lied shows how the dedication can invoke the performer's persona. The youthful cellist Lisa Cristiani appealed to salon audiences with her elegant playing, her engaging personality, and her beauty—as well as her Stradivari instrument. When she was seventeen, Mendelssohn performed with her at a Leipzig concert, so he knew her style and her persona (MacGregor 2001, 6:667). We could well say that the Lied ohne Worte gives a voice to a lyric cellist's persona, feminine and charming; the dedication reinforces this understanding.

MUSIC: INTERNAL EVIDENCE FOR THE NARRATIVE VOICE

I would now like to turn to some cases in which the music itself might direct us to the narrative voice in a movement or work. It can do this in any of several ways. For example:

- *A particular idiom* may govern the work, a recognisable quality or manner that can be attributed to a certain kind of voice. The

Lied for the cello represents this sort of situation, although in the case of a Lied ohne Worte the voice is that of a lyric persona, the *lyrisches ich*, rather than a narrator.[18]

- Intrusion into the piece's plot of some *music that clearly does not participate in the action*, often a passage that serves as either frame or commentary. We shall discover what I have come to regard as an instance of this in a quite unexpected place.
- Establishment of the identity of the narrative voice by *quotation* or *allusion* within the piece to a specific repertoire of music. In a moment I shall try to illustrate this by means of the C-minor Trio.

THE VOICE EMERGING FROM MUSIC EXTERNAL TO THE PLOT

First, I would like to go all the way back to the first movement of the C-minor Piano Quartet, op. 1, which, because of its early date and references to Enlightenment and early Restoration composers, we would surely imagine a most unlikely candidate for this sort of methodology.

The crucial moment here, to my way of hearing, comes at the close of the movement. A coda, which frames the plot of a piece, can assume a narrative function if its music stands apart from the characters in the action. Quite strikingly, that occurs here (see figure 9). Beginning at bar 286 the piano has a passage that appears as a brief voice-leading illustration, where the outer voices relate as a sequence of intervals in contrary motion as sixths and thirds. We might be hearing a brief illustration of invertible counterpoint between soprano and bass, filled out with arpeggiated chords. In bar 290 there follows a very obvious demonstration of a Corellian chain of 7-6 suspensions between violin and viola, set over the same bass and harmonic progression that we just heard four bars earlier. It seems remarkably "composerly" and not at all like anything in the body of the movement's plot.

18. Since this is a relatively straightforward matter, it seems unnecessary to multiply or interrogate additional instances.

Figure 9. Piano Quartet in C minor, op. 1 (MWV Q11), movement 1, bars 286–300

Surely we cannot help but perceive the intrusion of a composer, and particularly a rather self-conscious one, at the moment when the music tells us, "The story has concluded."

More than that, the last few bars, the final assertion of the movement, consist harmonically of no more than dominant and tonic chords (bars 295–300). Melodically, they take up the rising C-minor triad from the very first bar of the work, but fortissimo and in rhythmic diminution. The coda thus asserts possession of the material. It appears to insist, "I am the teller of this story."

Taking this together with the musical allusions to Mozart and Rossini, as well as the musical plot that gives the Viennese Classic composer priority over the Restoration Italian, we understand the narrative persona as both classically skilled and Classic in predilections. This would, of course, apply to Mendelssohn himself in the mid-1820s, so Ernst Wolff did not have it quite right when he wrote of this movement that "In its musical sentiment it bears no particularly distinctive traces that one could actually call Mendelssohnian" (Wolff 1909, 28, my translation).[19] It is important, though, to remember that the persona does not have complete congruence with the person of Felix Mendelssohn Bartholdy; persona and composer merely share some tastes and viewpoints. Neither of the two represents the other fully; two works or movements by the same composer may have different narrative voices; and the persona of a given piece might differ from or disagree with the composer himself, even diametrically.

IDENTIFYING THE VOICE THROUGH MUSICAL QUOTATION OR ALLUSION

Let us now consider a movement that we have not yet discussed—the finale of the C-minor Piano Trio, the last of Mendelssohn's multi-movement chamber works for strings and piano. Table 7 shows the movement's outline. The rhythmic/melodic style of the P theme (see figure 10) establishes the setting and character

19. "Es trägt in der musikalischen Erfindung keine besonders eigenartigen Züge, die man etwa Mendelssohnisch nennen könnte, . . . "

as unmistakably Italian; it is a saltarello (bars 1–8). The S theme adopts a character at once more lyrical and bolder in E♭ major (bars 49–52). In the middle of the rising action of section 3 a new theme intrudes (see figure 11). Not only does it have a completely different style, but it paraphrases two chorale melodies, "Gelobet seist Du, Jesu Christ" and "Herr Gott, Dich loben alle wir,"[20] first in chordal texture (bars 129–49) and then in a sort of cantus firmus setting (bars 149–67), identifying a presence external to the plot and one, moreover, that asserts its character as German and Lutheran. Further, as contrasted to the spirit of the rest of the music, this presence brings with it a feeling of meditative contemplation.

This theme gives way to a return of the buoyant saltarello (bar 171). At the arrival of the coda the character of the chorale changes, so that it now appears triumphantly to have seized control of the action (bar 267). The saltarello theme is brought into this sphere, but S begins tamely (bar 297) and only gradually leads to a final stretta.

In some ways this movement resembles the first movement plot of the B-minor Piano Quartet op. 3, where an intrusive presence appears late and then assumes a kind of independent fulfilment at the end. I want to suggest, however, that the new theme here remains more external to the action, so that we might do well to consider other elements of the C-minor Trio as a whole that would lead us to perceive the presence of a narrating voice.

The first such evidence comes in the nature of the first movement. As we have seen, its plot depends on the exploration of potentialities in the main character that arise from its contrapuntal treatment in canon and in augmentation. This contrapuntalism in itself must draw our attention to the presence behind the action. We inevitably notice that the presentation of the plot comes from a voice that is unusually composerly.

20. For a discussion of the details of this paraphrase, see Schmidt[-Beste] (1996, 324–27). (Schmidt-Beste also notes a somewhat more obscure resemblance of the close of Mendelssohn's invented chorale melody to "Lobt Gott, Ihr Christen alle gleich.")

Form division	Plot contour	Harmonic level	Musical material	Thematic character	Bar numbers
Part I	Stable situation	c	P	Saltarello	1
Section 1	Increasing tension				
Section 2	Contrasting situation	E♭	S	Bold	49
Part II	Rising action to	Relatively stable: E♭	Development of P	Saltarello	87, 106b
Section 3	climax	→ c	N (+ P)	Lutheran, meditative	129
		A♭			
Section 4	Resolution and denouement	Arrival of c (very subtle)	P	Saltarello	175b
		c	S	Bold	201
			Development of P	Saltarello (with imitation by inversion)	251
Coda		C	N	Lutheran, triumphant	267
		C	S fragment	Now relaxed	297
		C	P	Saltarello	327–53

Table 7. Form of Mendelssohn, Piano Trio in C minor, op. 66 (MWV Q33), movement 4

Figure 10. Piano Trio in C minor, op. 66 (MWV Q33), movement 4, bars 1–8

Second, in the scherzo that forms the third movement of the C-minor Trio an odd interruption pops in at bar 13, contrasting with the perpetual-motion sixteenth-notes of the main idea. This intrusive motive, a pair of descending triads in dactylic rhythm, starting on D minor, sounds oddly familiar. In fact, it strongly resembles the principal theme of the D-minor Trio's finale, in very much the same tempo (we might compare both the first bars and bars 6–8 of op. 49 mvt. 4 to bars 13–16 of op. 66 mvt. 3).

Cumulatively, this combination of musical features yields an unusually recognisable self-representation of the narrative persona. We hear the voice behind the action altogether as being that of a craftsmanly composer—rather than of, for example, a "hero" or a "Romantic dreamer." Further, the piece connects

Figure 11. Piano Trio in C minor, op. 66 (MWV Q33), movement 4, bars 129–38

itself by musical reference to the op. 49 Piano Trio, which we know to have been composed by Felix Mendelssohn Bartholdy. Finally, the controlling presence in the last movement asserts itself as German and Lutheran. We will naturally imagine the voice in the C-minor Trio as that of its actual composer—or at least of someone whose personality and experience share much with those of Mendelssohn.

This sort of explicit self-identification of the musical narrator with specific traits of the biographical composer remains extremely rare, and we should certainly approach this sort of conclusion very cautiously, for to assert that the music expresses the ideas specifically of the person writing the music tends to encourage hearing the piece as if it did not embody a broadly conceived subjectivity with which we as listeners can identify. It risks narrowing the voice so closely as to make the work merely diaristic and so potentially trivial. Most Romantic narratives come from fictive and more idealised narrative positions, and it is precisely this that opens the understanding of the work of art as both expansive and broadly meaningful to many listeners.

CONCLUSIONS

To conclude, I would simply like to review some important issues and offer some comments about the principles that have guided this discussion. First, we cannot remind ourselves too often or too emphatically that plot and narrative do not mean the same thing. A work that unfolds a plot need not be narrative in the strict or strong sense of the latter term. Narrative builds on plot, in the sense that music enacts the plot. The quality of narrativity depends on our awareness of the narrative voice, which serves the function of presenting that action (or even of critiquing it).

Second, we can approach the project of identifying voice in music in a variety of methodological ways. External (paratextual/paramusical) indications of voicedness can arise from the composer's deliberate additions to a work, or they can come from reception history. They should not, however, rely on the composer's biography. That is to say, while biographical information might suggest to us certain aspects of a narrative persona, we must not confuse the narrator with the composer. Internal (musical) factors may also reveal the narrative voice. These might include distinctive musical idioms, hypertextual references, or moments foreign to the plot.

Finally, one might ask why plot and narrative matter—why we cannot satisfy ourselves with analysis of musical form and with the biography of the composer. I would answer that narrative constitutes a powerful means of musical understanding, unmatched by standard means of analysis and biography.

The discovery of musical plot does, of course, represent a type of analysis. Unlike more conventional approaches, however, it helps to avoid some analytical errors. For one thing, it aids us in resisting the inclination to treat pieces as static structures; instead it forces us to understand them as temporal and processual experiences. As a corollary to that, it reminds us that the task of critical analysis should not merely lead to a correct classification of the designs of musical works or moments within them, based on established templates, but to a compelling reading. Following the plot of a work opens up understanding of the work's idiosyncrasies, which thus become its central sites of meaning, rather than seeming to be errors or random eccentricities. Further, it makes us aware of the functions that different musical materials serve in shaping, or changes that they undergo in experiencing, the course of the music, so that we do not perceive themes as placeholders in a framework but as having agency in the plot.

Narrativity represents a central principle (I would assert, *the* central principle) of Romanticism, because it locates an individual subject behind the communicative action of a musical work. Nineteenth-century audiences and critics regarded the identification of the voice as crucial to the appreciation of the music. For a short work such as a song or character piece, as for a shorter poem, this presence is the lyric ego. For a long work, including a plotted movement or sometimes a multi-movement cyclic work, it is the narrative voice.

Mendelssohn's chamber music stands in a challenging position for us in regard to narrativity. In that it relies fully on the concept of plottedness, as do works throughout nineteenth-century music, it belongs fundamentally to the post-Enlightenment and post-Classic episteme and aesthetic. Only in certain places, and somewhat tentatively, does the narrative voice emerge. To unveil the persona lurking in these movements requires alertness to widely varied kinds of external and internal clues, sharp-eared listening, and a receptive imagination that integrates the unexpected into a more multi-layered understanding of the music. These quartets and trios may seem unlikely instances, yet in their own subtle ways they do, after all, reward narrative interpretation.

REFERENCES

Abbate, Carolyn. 1989. "What the Sorcerer Said." *19th-Century Music* 12 (3): 221–30.

Almén, Byron. 2008. *A Theory of Musical Narrative*. Bloomington: Indiana University Press.

Aristotle. 1987. *Poetics*. Translated by Richard Janko. Indianapolis: Hackett.

Bakhtin, Mikhail M. 1981. *The Dialogic Imagination: Four Essays*. Edited by Michael Holquist. Translated by Caryl Emerson and Michael Holquist. Austin: University of Texas Press. First published 1975 as *Voprosy literatury i èstetiki* (Moscow: Hudožestvennaâ literatura).

Cavell, Stanley. (1969) 2002. *Must We Mean What We Say?* Updated ed. Cambridge: Cambridge University Press. First published 1969 (New York: Scribner).

Cone, Edward T. 1974. *The Composer's Voice*. Berkeley: University of California Press.

Dahlhaus, Carl. 1991. *Ludwig van Beethoven: Approaches to His Music*. Translated by Mary Whittall. New York: Oxford University Press. First published 1987 as *Ludwig van Beethoven und seine Zeit* (Laaber: Laaber-Verlag).

Dwight's Journal of Music. 1853. "Concerts of the Past Week." *Dwight's Journal of Music* 2 (15): 117–19.

Foucault, Michel. 1971. *The Order of Things: An Archaeology of the Human Sciences*. New York: Pantheon. First published 1966 as *Les mots et les choses: Une archéologie des sciences humaines* (Paris: Gallimard).

Hatten, Robert. 1991. "On Narrativity in Music: Expressive Genres and Levels of Discourse in Beethoven." *Indiana Theory Review* 12: 75–98.

Hepokoski, James, and Warren Darcy. 2006. *Elements of Sonata Theory: Norms, Types, and Deformations in the Late-Eighteenth-Century Sonata*. Oxford: Oxford University Press.

Jordan, Roland, and Emma Kafalenos. 1989. "The Double Trajectory: Ambiguity in Brahms and Henry James." *19th-Century Music* 13 (2), 129–44.

Kivy, Peter. 2002. *Introduction to a Philosophy of Music*. Oxford: Oxford University Press / Clarendon Press.

———. 2009. *Antithetical Arts: On the Ancient Quarrel between Literature and Music*. Oxford: Oxford University Press / Clarendon Press.

Kollmann, August F. 1799. *An Essay on Practical Musical Composition, According to the Nature of That Science and the Principles of the Greatest Musical Authors*. London.

Kramer, Lawrence. 1990. "'As If a Voice Were in Them': Music, Narrative, and Deconstruction." Chap. 6 in *Music as Cultural Practice, 1800–1900*. Berkeley: University of California Press.

LaRue, Jan. 1970. *Guidelines for Style Analysis*. New York: Norton. Revised as LaRue 1992.

———. 1992. *Guidelines for Style Analysis*. 2nd ed. Warren, MI: Harmonie Park Press. Originally published as LaRue 1970.

Liszka, James Jakób. 1989. *The Semiotic of Myth: A Critical Study of the Symbol*. Bloomington: Indiana University Press.

MacGregor, Lynda. 2001. "Cristiani, Lisa (Barbier)." In *The New Grove Dictionary of Music and Musicians*, edited by Stanley Sadie, 2nd ed., 6:667. London: Macmillan.

Maus, Fred Everett. 1988. "Music as Drama." *Music Theory Spectrum* 10: 56–73.

———. 2001. "Narratology, narrativity." In *The New Grove Dictionary of Music and Musicians*, edited by Stanley Sadie, 2nd ed., 17:641–43. London: Macmillan.

Nattiez, Jean-Jacques. 1990. "Can One Speak of Narrativity in Music?" *Journal of the Royal Musical Association* 115 (2): 240–57.

Newcomb, Anthony. 1984. "Once More 'Between Absolute and Program Music': Schumann's Second Symphony." *19th-Century Music* 7 (3): 233–50.

———. 1987. "Schumann and Late Eighteenth-Century Narrative Strategies." *19th-Century Music* 11 (2), 164–74.

———. 1992. "Narrative Archetypes and Mahler's Ninth Symphony." In *Music and Text: Critical Inquiries*, edited by Stephen Paul Scher, 118–36. Cambridge: Cambridge University Press.

Niemöller, Klaus Wolfgang. 2004. "Gattungstradition und neue Ausdrucksdramaturgie in den Klaviertrios von Felix Mendelssohn-Bartholdy." In *Dem Stolz und der Zierde unserer Stadt: Felix Mendelssohn Bartholdy und Leipzig*, Proceedings of the Erstes Mendelssohn-Fest, IX. Internationales Gewandhaus-Symposium 1, edited by Wilhelm Seidel, 261–72. Leipzig: Peters.

Propp, Vladimir. 1968. *Morphology of the Folktale*. Austin: University of Texas Press.

Ratner, Leonard. 1980. *Classic Music: Expression, Form, and Style*. New York: Schirmer.

[Rellstab?, Ludwig]. 1824. Review of *Quatuor pour le Piano-Forte, avec accompagnement de Violon, Alto et Violoncelle, composé etc. par Felix Mendelssohn-Bartholdy, Oeuvr. I. Berliner allgemeine musikalische Zeitung* 1 (19) (12 May): 168.

Rellstab, Ludwig. 1825. Review of Felix Mendelssohn Bartholdy, *Drittes Quartett für Fortepiano, Violine, Viola und Violoncell, . . . Goethe gewidmet . . . . Berliner allgemeine musikalische Zeitschrift* 2: 354.

Rosen, Charles. 1971. *The Classical Style: Haydn, Mozart, Beethoven*. New York: Norton.

———. (1980) 1988. *Sonata Forms*. Rev. ed. New York: Norton. First published 1980.

Schering, Arnold. 1934. *Beethoven in neuer Deutung*. Leipzig: C. F. Kahnt.

———. (1936) 1973. *Beethoven und die Dichtung: Mit einer Einleitung zur Geschichte und Ästhetik der Beethovendeutung*. Hildesheim: G. Olms. First published 1936 (Berlin: Junker und Dünnhaupt).

Schmidt, J. P. 1824. Review of *Quatuor pour le Piano-Forte, avec Accomp. de Violon, Alto et Violoncelle, composé et dedié à son Altesse, Monseigneur le Prince Antoine Radzivil, etc. par Felix Mendelssohn-Bartholdy,* Oeuv. 1. *Allgemeine musikalische Zeitung* 26 (12) (18 March): 184.

Schmidt[-Beste], Thomas Christian. 1996. *Die ästhetischen Grundlagen der Instrumentalmusik Felix Mendelssohn Bartholdys*. Stuttgart: M und P, Verlag für Wissenschaft und Forschung.

Scholes, Robert, and Robert Kellogg. 1966. *The Nature of Narrative*. New York: Oxford University Press.

Schumann, Robert. 1946. *On Music and Musicians*. Edited by Konrad Wolff. Translated by Paul Rosenfeld. New York: Pantheon. First published 1854 in *Gesammelte Schriften über Musik und Musiker* (Leipzig: Georg Wigand).

Seaton, Douglass. 2010. *Ideas and Styles in the Western Musical Tradition*. 3rd ed. New York: Oxford University Press.

———. 2011. Review of *A Theory of Musical Narrative*, by Byron Almén. *Journal of Musicological Research* 30 (1): 72–76.

Souchay, Marc-André, and Felix Mendelssohn. 1998. "An Exchange of Letters." In *Source Readings in Music History*, edited by Oliver

Strunk, rev. ed., general editor Leo Treitler, 1198–201. New York: Norton. Also published in a 7 vol. ed.

Todd, R. Larry. 2003. *Mendelssohn: A Life in Music*. Oxford: Oxford University Press.

Wingfield, Paul, and Julian Horton. 2012. "Norm and Deformation in Mendelssohn's Sonata Forms." In *Mendelssohn Perspectives*, edited by Nicole Grimes and Angela R. Mace, 83–112. Farnham, UK: Ashgate.

Wolff, Ernst. 1909. *Felix Mendelssohn Bartholdy*. 2nd ed. Berlin: Harmonie.

ROBERT SCHUMANN'S POETIC PARAPHRASES
ANALYTICAL IMPLICATIONS

Hubert Moßburger

STAATLICHE HOCHSCHULE FÜR MUSIK
UND DARSTELLENDE KUNST STUTTGART

SCHUMANN'S CONCEPT OF "THE POETIC" (DAS POETISCHE)

"The poetic" is the central category in Schumann's aesthetics of music. Before we inquire into the meaning of poetic paraphrases and their importance for modern analysis, we have to consider Schumann's concept of the poetic. This includes three aspects. First, the poetic is the shared substance of the different arts. For Schumann (1946), "the aesthetic principle is the same in every art; only the material differs" (44).[1] The same aesthetic substance can be expressed by different points of view or senses in music, in a poem, or in a picture. It follows that it must be possible to translate an aesthetic subject from one art to the other: the poetic content of a musical work can be also expressed through another suitable art form, such as poetry, for example. But the Romantic generation believed that music is the highest of all the arts, because music can express the unspoken. "Tones are higher words" (Töne sind höhere Worte), Schumann noted in his diary (1971, 96, my translation).

This leads us to the second aspect of the poetic: it makes the unspoken sensible. Music elevates specific external content to higher realms of poetry by transforming the inexplicable into an essence that can only be understood through feelings, feelings that are beyond the grasp of words. Here words end, and the language of music begins. Transcendence is a special feature of the poetic in music.

1. "Die Ästhetik der einer Kunst ist die der andern; nur das Material ist verschieden" (Schumann 1914, 1:26).

Third, the predicate "the poetic" is the highest aesthetic value judgement that Schumann gives as a critic. To be worthy of his praise, a composition should be able to evoke a poetic state in the player or listener. The poetic is the opposite of the prosaic, which is mechanical, trivial, average, and purely a matter of craft. In a positive sense the poetic is original, fantastical, new, unusual, secret, unknown, special, individual, and—all in all—Romantic.

THE RECEPTION OF THE POETIC

In summary, Schumann's concept of the poetic means the unity of all art, the transcended essence of extra-musical content, and the opposite of everything prosaic. But how does this idea of the poetic function? It can be described as a correlation between inspiration, composition, and reception, as figure 1 illustrates:

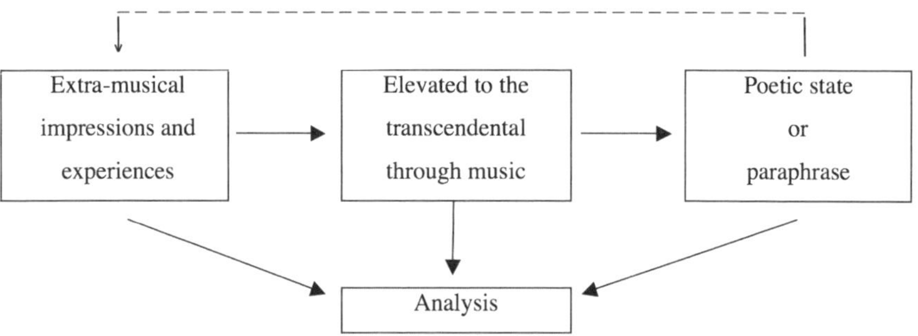

Figure 1. The reception of the poetic

For Schumann, music can be unconsciously inspired by accidental influences from outside; "The greater the number of elements cognate in music, which the thought or picture created in tones contains, the more poetic and plastic the expression of the composition" (Schumann 1946, 181).[2] These elements can be of different kinds. Schumann says that he is affected by everything

2. "Je mehr nun der Musik verwandte Elemente die mit den Tönen erzeugten Gedanken oder Gebilde in sich tragen, von je poetischerem oder plasticherem Ausbrucke die Composition sein" (Schumann 1835b, 50).

that happens in the world—politics, literature, people; and he thinks about all this in his own way, so this pent-up tension must find an outlet through his music. The content of these influences should be not prosaic but poetic. For Schumann, this is the reason why his compositions are so difficult to understand, but also why they are so significant. He wrote self-confidently to Clara Wieck on 13 April 1838:

> That's why many of my compositions are so difficult to understand; they relate to distant, often significant concerns because all the strange things in this age touch me, and I must express them musically.
>
> That's also why so few [new] compositions satisfy me because, aside from all the technical faults, they indulge in musical sentiments of the lowest order, in ordinary lyrical effusions, etc.; the best that can be achieved that way does not even approach the beginning of my musical world. The former may be a flower, but the latter is a more inspired poem; the former is a primitive impulse, but the latter is a work of poetic consciousness. (Schumann and Schumann 1984–87, 1:150)[3]

These external influences, which are poetic, are not simply reflected unchanged in the music, as they are in the prosaic musical painting of an imitative aesthetic. In fact, the external influences are elevated through music to a higher domain, which is "the higher power of poetry" (die höhere Potenz der Poesie), as Schumann says (1971, 96, my translation). On this higher level, the unspoken—which can only be expressed through music—will be distilled from the influences, impressions, and feelings and made still more poetic by music, the language of the soul.

---

3. "Deshalb sind auch viele meiner Compositionen so schwer zu verstehen, weil sie an entfernte Interessen anknüpfen, oft auch bedeutend, weil mich alles Merkwürdige der Zeit ergreift, und ich es dann musikalisch wieder aussprechen muß. Darum genügen mir auch so wenig [neuere] Compositionen, weil sie abgesehen von allen Mängeln des Handwerks sich auch in musikalischen Empfindungen der niedrigsten Gattung, in gewöhnlichen lyrischen Ausrufungen herumtreiben; das Höchste was hier geleistet werden kann reicht noch nicht bis zum Anfang der Welt meiner Musik. Jenes kann eine Blume sein, dieses ist das um so viel geistigere Gedicht; jenes ein Trieb der rohen Natur, dieses ein Werk des dichterischen Bewußtseins" (Schumann and Schumann 1984–2001, 1:146).

The transcendental effect of these influences, elevated through music, puts the listener or the musician into a poetic state, which can give rise to a poetic paraphrase. This should not be a prosaic re-creation, but—in an ideal case—an aesthetic product coequal with the music. For Schumann, the highest response makes the same impression as the work that prompted it. In consequence, reading a companion poem by Jean Paul can lead to a better understanding of a symphony by Beethoven than reading "a dozen art critics" (die Dutzend-Kunstrichtler) (Schumann 1835a, 42, my translation). A poetic equivalent may recall the composer's original influences, or even be identical in effect, in the case of a Romantic consonance of souls or a modern recipient who is aware of the original sources (see the dashed arrow in figure 1). But this need not be the case, because Schumann requires that both composer and recipient be open in their approach to poetic interpretation. The composer should not patronise the listener with a detailed programme; the imagination of the recipient should be allowed to develop freely. The exact content that the music expresses is not as important as the question of whether a composition is ever able to evoke a poetic state. And it also does not matter whether a composer receives extra-musical inspiration before or after the composition of the work. It is only to defend his music against accusations of prosaic imitation that Schumann emphasises that his poetic titles are added *after* the composition has been completed. For Schumann, these titles provide "nothing more than tiny finger-posts to the interpretation and conception" (Schumann 1907, 133).[4] And this is exactly what is meant by the poetic: it must only exist as suggestion and intuition. So it rests between absolute and programme music. And poetic paraphrases are intended as attempts to transfer the unspoken to the imagination, which activates the other arts to gain a deeper understanding.

4. "weiter nichts als feinere Fingerzeige für Vortrag und Auffassung" (Schumann 1904, 170). Letter to Heinrich Dorn, 5 September 1839.

POETIC AND ANALYTICAL IMPLICATIONS

What does this kind of poetic reception mean for modern analysis? First of all we must state that the Romantic conception of music was in its very essence an aesthetic of poetic reflection (Tadday 1999, 213). So if we want to deal with Romantic music in a historically analytical way, we cannot ignore this and rely only upon the methods of structural analysis. But how can we reconcile the Romantic mode of reception with modern analysis? Creating a poetic equivalent is "easier said than done" (leichter gesagt als getan), Schumann confessed (1835a, 42, my translation), and it requires one whose poetic skill matches the composer's musical abilities. Today most of us could not achieve this, and we would not be taken very seriously if we produced a poem instead of an analysis. But we can look at the composer's own poetic paraphrases and see what analytic implications they have and how they can give us a deeper insight into his works.

Before we examine Schumann's poetic paraphrases and their analytical implications, we must go backwards from technical terms to their implicit aesthetic ideas, so we can retranslate the poetic paraphrases into our usual analytical language. This gives us the opportunity to find a midpoint between the two extremes of poetic and analytical language. A first step towards finding such a midpoint is the awareness that many music-theoretical terms already carry aesthetically relevant implications. For example, the contrasts between consonant and dissonant, diminished and augmented, or minor and major are aesthetic sound-qualities; the augmented fifth chord can have the meaning of too much sorrow, of a feeling of enthusiasm, or of a distortion or overstatement of reality. For Arnold Schoenberg (1978), modulation is an "activity" which serves as "a reflection of our own human enterprise" (151). Enharmonic change has been equated with relationships or feelings since the eighteenth century, by writers like Rousseau, C. P. E. Bach, Marpurg, and Daube. It seems that the first attempts to translate music into words really were influenced by the emotional content.

Some terms seem to have neutral, purely technical meanings. But most of them have lost their meaning in the course of history. If we look back, we see that these supposedly "dead concepts" (Paul 1973, 15) have their roots in the musico-rhetorical theory of figures (Figurenlehre) of the seventeenth century. They lost their affective qualities with their translation into other languages, especially German. Figure 2 provides some examples of this neutralisation of meaning through translation:

Musico-rhetorical term	Modern term: German (English)
Passus duriusculus (hard walk, lamento bass)	Chromatische(r) Schritt(e) (chromatic step[s])
Relatio non harmonica (disharmonious relation)	Querstand (false relation—literally "cross-position")
Fauxbourdon ("false")	Sextakkordkette, -mixtur (mixture or chain of sixth chords)
Interrogation (a questioning figure)	phrygischer Halbschluss (Phrygian half-cadence)
Noema (a significant "thought")	homophoner Satz (homophonic passage)
Abruptio (a sudden interruption)	Pauze (rest)
Climax oder Gradatio (increase)	Sequenz (sequence)
Exclamatio (exclamation)	kleiner Sextsprung aufwärts (minot sixth upwards)
Pathopoeia (sorrow, affect)	tonartfremder Ton (chromatic tone)
Plorant semiton (tearful semitone)	Halbttonschritt (semitone step)

Figure 2. Neutralisation of the original meanings

To reach an appropriate historical analysis of Romantic music, we can take a middle route between the two extremes of technical analysis and poetic paraphrase. I call the language of this kind of analysis "musico-linguistic imagery." Figure 3 illustrates the relationship between the three analytical methods:

---

technical language → musico-linguistic imagery ← poetic paraphrase

---

Figure 3. Three analytical methods

We can take the aesthetic implications of the specific technical language and use them to create metaphors that describe the effect or aesthetic of the music appropriately. In contrast with pure poetic paraphrase, musico-linguistic imagery is based directly or indirectly on aspects of the musical structure. So it provides us with a good present-day mediation between purely structural and purely poetic descriptions of music and also with a useful method for analysing Romantic music.

These three linguistic areas—technical analysis, musico-linguistic imagery, and poetic paraphrase—will now be applied to the chord progression A♭–a♭–E^6 (figure 4):

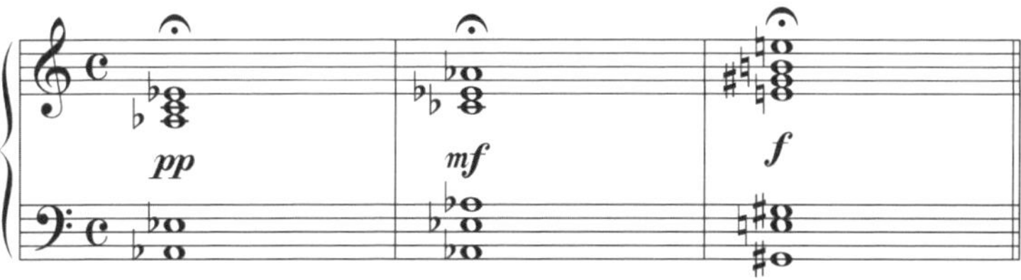

Figure 4. Chord progression for analysis

In the technical language of German functional theory this could be analysed as T–$t \approx tG_3$ (A♭: I, i, VI/i). To put this into words: first, the A♭ major chord is played *pianissimo* in the bass register and with the pedal depressed (so that the other strings of the piano can resonate); this is followed by the minor variant, played *mezzo forte*, and then a *Leittonwechselklang* of A♭ minor (the first inversion of E-major), played *forte*, which is enharmonically changed from F♭ to E, perhaps to avoid additional accidentals. The enharmonic submediant motion from A♭ major to E major is mediated by A♭ minor, a chord more closely related to both, which enables a *Leittonwechselklang*. The voice-leading enables a gradual transformation by two successive chromatic degrees (C–C♭ and E♭–E).

An equivalent musico-linguistic account is anchored by technical terms and describes the musical effects without providing a detailed programme. For example, it might run as follows: the A♭ major chord, with a bright major third but a shaded key-colour, is struck very softly in the dark bass register; while the chord dies away, the resonance effected by the depressed pedal causes the triad to dissolve into a mysterious sound of nature, which ushers in another world. The A minor chord darkens the dying sound further, although it is played more loudly and in a higher register; in direct contrast to its major variant, the exposed minor chord evokes all the traditional expressions of sadness, sorrow, pain, and so on. With only one changed pitch, a bright shining and sonorous, but floating and fragile, first-inversion chord sounds stronger and higher than the preceding two. But in relation to the first chord, the mediant is now far removed. The broken context is shown in the enharmonic change from a dark (flat) to a bright (sharp) tonal region. The bright chord takes the past darkness upon itself and seems to be internally riven. The unstable and enharmonically ambiguous F♭/E first-inversion chord is still tonally fragile; it must be affirmed further in the future.

Finally, here is an example of poetic paraphrase taken from "Kreisler's Musico-Poetic Club," written by E. T. A. Hoffmann:

> Pianissimo, and with the dampers raised, Kreisler then played a full A flat major chord in the bass. To the diminishing whisper of the notes, he spoke: "What strange and magical susurration rises all around me? Invisible wings flutter up and down; I swim through the fragrant ether. But the fragrance radiates in flaming, mysteriously intertwining circles. They are propitious spirits, moving their golden wings in sounds and chords of surpassing beauty."
>
> A flat minor chord (*mezzo forte*)
>
> "Ah! They carry me to the land of eternal yearning, but as they take hold of me, pain awakens and tries to burst forth from my breast by rending it asunder."
>
> E major, first inversion chord (*ancora più forte*)
>
> "Stand firm, my heart! Do not break under the searing heat that suffuses my breast. Be of good cheer, my sturdy spirit! Rise up, and

make your presence felt in the element that gave you birth, that is your home!" (Hoffman 1989, 132–33)[5]

Even if we did not know which chords Kreisler was playing, we could still make a good guess at what follows the first chord. We can see what is implied musically by the change of mood from the exalted, glorious chord (A♭ major), to one of pain (minor variant), and then by the danger of breast and heart being torn apart (enharmonic change), and finally by the optimistic and rising spirit (brighter sound in the transition from the flat to the sharp area). With this paraphrase, we can see how musico-linguistic images form the missing link between purely technical and purely poetic language (indicated by the arrows in figure 3).

Musico-linguistic images correlate with Schumann's idea of the poetic as the shared substance of the arts—here, of music, poetry, and fine art. Metaphors can say more than "dead concepts," as Jean Paul says: "The essence of poetic presentation, like all life, can be represented only by a second poetic presentation. . . . Even mere similes can often express more than literal explanations. . . . At least images would mirror kindred life better than do dead concepts" (Paul 1973, 15).[6] Conversely, musico-linguistic imagery sharpens our view of the analytic implications found in the poetic paraphrases of the Romantic generation. We

5. "Kreisler griff nun pianissimo mit gehobenen Dämpfern im Baß den vollen As-Dur-Akkord. Sowie die Töne versäuselten, sprach er: Was rauscht denn so wunderbar, so seltsam um mich her?—Unsichtbare Fittiche wehen auf und nieder—ich schwimme im duftigen Äther.—Aber der Duft erglänzt in flammenden, geheimnisvoll verschlungenen Kreisen. Holde Geister sind es, die die goldnen Flügel regen in überschwenglich herrlichen Klängen und Akkorden.

Ach!—sie tragen mich ins Land der ewigen Sehnsucht, aber wie sie mich erfassen, erwacht der Schmerz und will aus der Brust entfliehen, indem er sie gewaltsam zerreißt.

Halt dich standhaft, mein Herz!—brich nicht, berührt von dem sengenden Strahl, der die Brust durchdrang.—Frisch auf, mein wackrer Geist!—rege und hebe dich empor in dem Element, das dich gebar, das deine Heimat ist!" (Hoffmann [1810–14] 1993, 77). The quotation is only the beginning of a paraphrase for the entire twelve-chord sequence.

6. "Das Wesen der dichterischen Darstellung ist wie alles Leben nur durch eine zweite darzustellen. . . . Sogar bloße Gleichnisse können oft mehr als Worterklärungen aussagen. . . . Wenigstens würde in Bildern sich das verwandte Leben besser spiegeln, als in toten Begriffen" (Paul 1804, 1–2). This quotation can be found nearly complete in Schumann's collection of mottos (Schumann 1998, 142).

need only translate them back and anchor them in the musical structure. And we can assume that a poetic paraphrase might hide some more information deep inside its poetic transformation. From this point of view, we can also use poetic paraphrase as a guide for structural analysis.

SCHUMANN'S TYPES OF POETIC PARAPHRASE

Many different kinds of poetic paraphrases were created by Schumann. We can find them in his reviews, in his aphorisms, letters, and diaries, and—compressed to one word—in his poetic titles. And we must distinguish between Schumann's own paraphrases and the poetic mottos or stories that he borrows from other authors. But it is difficult to find an original poetic paraphrase by Schumann about his own work. There are only a few scattered brief remarks, and the only one that is more detailed is not Schumann's own paraphrase; it is the old story of Hero and Leander, which fits the character and form of the *Phantasiestück* "In der Nacht," op. 12 (see Tadday 1999, 140–42). Because Schumann didn't write reviews of his own works, we have to examine his poetic paraphrases of the music of *other* composers.

The kind of review Schumann writes depends on the quality of a composition: if it is not good, he uses technical language to set out its mistakes exactly; but if the music is "poetic," it earns a poetic review. For example, consider Schubert; while listening to his music, Schumann imagined a "novel in tones" (Tonroman) (Schumann 1971, 96, my translation) or "a composed novel by Jean Paul" (einen komponierten Roman Jean Paul's) (Schumann 1885, 82, my translation). Conversely, Schumann's own compositional activity could take poetry as its stimulus, as with the *Papillons*, op. 2, which are known to have been inspired by the final chapter of Jean Paul's *Flegeljahre*.

In addition, there are many poetic paraphrases or aphorisms that Schumann created on the subjects of musical elements or concepts such as chords or keys. So we will first look at the poetic implications of music-theoretical ideas and then, conversely, at the analytical implications of Schumann's poetic paraphrases.

Expressive implications of music-theoretical ideas

The Romantic generation distrusted rational ways of understanding music. So Schumann (1904, 149) professed to have learned more counterpoint from Jean Paul than from his music teacher. Because he felt that music could be better understood with poetry than with music theory, Schumann poeticised technical terms. By using musico-linguistic imagery, he extracts astonishing implicit content from music-theoretical terms. Even the most elementary and conventional ideas gain some poetic meaning, especially such value-neutral musical "material" as triads or cadences. It is not the special or the unusual, but the common, that needs to be made Romantic. That is why Novalis proclaimed:

> The world must be romanticized. . . . By giving a lofty sense to what is common, a mysterious aspect to the everyday, the dignity of the unknown to the familiar, the appearance of infinity to the finite, I am romanticizing these things. (Translation from Rossbach 2008, 479)[7]

Here are some examples of Schumann's poeticising of music-theoretical ideas that were subsequently realised in compositions. Schumann associates consonant triads with metaphors from the areas of religion ("triad, holy word"), love ("this gentle harmonica-triad of life, this one: *I love you*"), time ("triad = times. Third bridges past and future, as does the present"), feelings ("all the strings of our human feelings are stretched to such a soft minor triad"), soul ("holy soul-chord"), or heart ("he would touch your heart with some of his chords").[8] Inspired by the apotheosis of

7. "Die Welt muß romantisiert werden. . . . Indem ich dem Gemeinen einen hohen Sinn, dem Gewöhnlichen ein geheimnisvolles Ansehn, dem Bekannten die Würde des Unbekannten, dem Endlichen einen unendlichen Schein gebe, so romantisiere ich es" (Novalis [1798] 1978, 334).
8. "Dreyklang, heiliges Wort" (Schumann 1971, 125, my translation); "diesen milden Harmonikadreyklang des Lebens, dieses: *Ich liebe dich*" (ibid., 100, my translation); "Dreiklang = Zeiten. Terz vermittelt Vergangenheit und Zukunft als Gegenwart" (Schumann 1914, 1:23, translation from Schumann 1946, 42); "alle Saiten unseres menschlichen Fühlens zu einem solchen weichen Mollaccord gespannt" (Schumann 1971, 75, my translation); "heiligen Seelenaccord" (ibid., 100, my translation); "Mit

the triad in E. T. A. Hoffmann's (1814) historical essay "Old and New Church Music" (Alte und neue Kirchenmusik), and well before Richard Wagner's symbolic use of diatonic triads in chromatic surroundings, Schumann used triads in his music as a representation of purification and transcendence.

Dissonant sounds are linked by Schumann with pain, desire, or unfulfilled dreams. This is especially true if they form the end of a piece, as do the dominant seventh chords in "Bittendes Kind" (*Kinderszenen*, op. 15, no. 4) or "Im wunderschönen Mai" (*Dichterliebe*, op. 48, no. 1).[9] In his diary, Schumann describes the impression of an organ improvisation that he heard late in the evening in a cathedral. At the end of this little essay, influenced by Jean Paul and E. T. A. Hoffmann, we find a poetic paraphrase of the dominant-seventh chord, which can stand as a Romantic testament to the aesthetic of the unresolved dissonance:

> The listeners fell silent – the strange organist finished – still one, two tones – now all becomes quiet – the moon fled shyly back – still a dissonant chord and nothing more – oh, our hearts longed for the mild consolation of the resolution; but no tone followed and all was silent. Silently the stranger rose, and silently the four men followed – Gustav said: And what then is our life but a seventh chord, full of doubt and containing only unfulfilled desires and unsatisfied hopes. The foreigner must have no small heart, to be able to close in such a way. (Schumann 1971, 138, my translation)[10]

---

manchen Accorden würde er Dir aber in's Herz dringen" (Schumann and Schumann 1984–2001, 2:473; translation from Schumann and Schumann 1984–87, 2:142).

9. In analysing *Dichterliebe*, Beate Julia Perrey (2003) attempts to synthesise music-analytical, literary-critical, philosophical, and psychoanalytical modes of thought.

10. "Sie [die Zuhörer] verstummten – der Fremde [Organist] schließt – Noch ein, zwey Töne – Jetzt wird Alles still – der Mond floh schüchtern zurük – noch ein dissonirender Accord u. keiner mehr – o da verlangten die Herzen nach dem milden Trost der Auflösung; aber kein Ton folgte nach u. Alles war stumm. Schweigend stand der Fremde auf, u. schweigend gingen die vier Menschen nach – Gustav sagte: Und was ist denn unser Leben auch weiter als ein zweifelvoller Septimenaccord, der nur unerfüllte Wünsche u. ungestillte Hoffnungen in sich führt. Der Fremde mußte kein kleines Herz haben, daß er so schließen konnte."

Musical implications of poetic language

Now we turn the previous section on its head and consider our main topic, the music-analytical implications of poetic language. In Schumann's poetic paraphrases there are different categories of music-theoretical passages: from pure poetry without any musical reference to paraphrases that are clearly anchored in the musical structure. Only in some of his long reviews (for example, of Hector Berlioz's *Symphonie fantastique* or Ferdinand Hiller's *Etüden für Pianoforte*, op. 15) does Schumann separate the poetic from the analytic part for reasons of pedagogy.

The first category—the poetic paraphrase with a greater or lesser use of musical terms—we can see for example in the "Mardi Gras Speech by Florestan (After a performance of Beethoven's Ninth Symphony)" (Schumann 1946, 99).[11] I quote the part where a concert visitor, who represents conservative taste and is called "cantor" by Florestan, the progressive, is shocked by the first chord of the finale, the opening of which Richard Wagner dubbed a "terror fanfare" (Schreckensfanfare) (Wagner 1873, 287, my translation).

> I said to a trembling man next to me: "What else is this chord, dear cantor, but a common chord with an anticipatory dominant-note in a somewhat complicated distribution, because one is uncertain whether to take the A of the timpani or the F of the bassoon for a bass? See Türk, part 19, page 7!" "Well, sir, you talk very loudly and certainly are not serious." Softly, yet with a terrible voice, I whispered: "Cantor, mind the thunderstorms. The lightning does not announce its visit by a butler; at the best it sends a storm before a thunderclap afterward. These are its ways." "But discords like that ought to be prepared —" But here the next one burst in. "Cantor, this beautiful seventh in the trumpets will forgive you." (Schumann 1946, 100)[12]

11. "Fastnachtsrede von Florestan Gehalten nach einer Auffürung der letzten Sinfonie von Beethoven" (Schumann 1914, 1:39).
12. "'Was ist er weiter, Kantor (sagte ich zu einem zitternden neben mir), als ein Dreiklang mit vorgehaltener Quinte in einer etwas verzwickten Versetzung, weil man nicht weiß, ob man das Pauken-A oder das Fagotten-F für Baßton nehmen soll? Sehen sie nur Türk, 19ter Theil, S. 7!'—'Ah, Herr sie sprechen sehr laut und spaßen

This ironical exchange refers to the first of the two "shock chords" and their free treatment of dissonance. First, Florestan tries to calm the trembling "cantor" by belittling the unprepared dissonance in the first bar of the finale. This chord, he assures him, is simply a triad with a suspended fifth in an ambiguous position. The cantor can reassure himself and find confirmation through music theory, for example that of Daniel Gottlob Türk. Then Florestan compares the unprepared dissonance to a thunderstorm, whose sudden lightning-bolts are not announced by a servant. Just as the philistine cantor tries spitefully to insist on the traditional rules of voice leading, another lightening bolt strikes. This second "shock chord" (bar 17), visible on the short score in figure 5, is different from the first one.

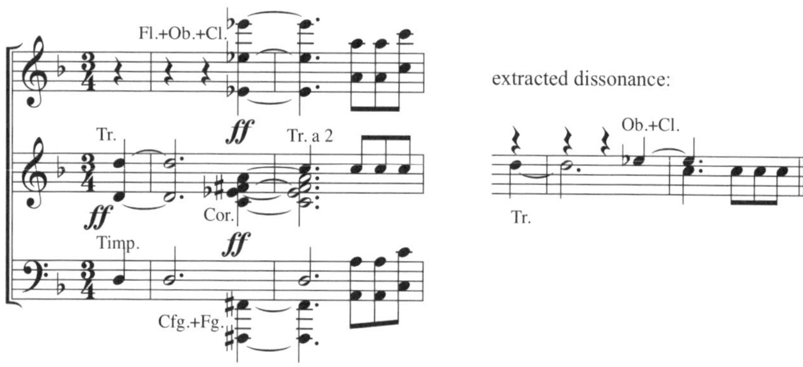

Figure 5. The second "shock chord" in the finale of Beethoven's Symphony No. 9 (bars 17–18)

Of the two clashing lines, the passive one in the trumpet is prepared, but the active one is left free (see the extracted dissonance in figure 5). In bar 18 the trumpet is the seventh of a ninth-chord,

bestimmt.'—Mit leiser, fürchterlicher Stimme sagte ich ihm ins Ohr: 'Kantor, nehmen Sie sich vor den Gewittern in acht! der Blitz schickt keinen Livreebedienten, eh' er einschlägt, höchstens einen Sturm vorher und drauf einen Donnerkeil. Das ist so seine Manier.'—'Vorbereitet müssen solche Dissonanzen dennoch'—da stürzte schon die andere herein. 'Kantor, die schöne Trompetenseptime vergibt euch'" (Schumann 1914, 1:40–41).

but it is also a resolution of the hard discord of the minor second d–e♭. Florestan's joke is that the "beautiful seventh," which is sinful in itself, awards the "te absolvo" to the cantor: partial resolution as a merely human gesture of forgiveness.

The second category of Schumann's poetic paraphrases encompasses those that are purely poetic without any technical terms. There are different degrees of poetic abstraction, from obvious imagery to highly cryptic esotericism. We can see this in the titles of Schumann's works, which are poetic paraphrases compressed to a single word and which offer only "tiny fingerposts to the interpretation and conception" (see above). For example, a title such as "Of Foreign Lands and Peoples" (Von fremden Ländern und Menschen) from the *Kinderszenen*, op. 15, no. 1, clearly leads the analyser towards the strange features that can be detected in the composition (here including the diminished seventh as an unexpected chord in the first bar, which hides the "foreign" B–A–C–H in its inner voice, or the strange mediant in bar 12 that concludes the chain of descending fifths). Highly cryptic in their poetic qualities are more generic titles like *Novelletten*, op. 21. Although Schumann suggested in a letter to Clara Wieck (6 February 1838) that his new work contains "humorous things, Egmont stories, family scenes with fathers, a wedding; in short, extremely charming things" (Schumann and Schumann 1984–87, 1:91),[13] this opus belongs to a group of compositions that were prompted by Clara Wieck and by Schumann's fight to win her.[14] Here all we can do is analyse the form of the musical narrative and speculate with these few fragments, which leave us alone with our own imagination.

In 1836 Schumann wrote a great and extended poetic paraphrase in the style of a scene with the "Davidsbündler." Let us look only at one short part of the whole and guess at the analytical implications it might have: "Two reapers waltzing together in a happy trance. He says softly, 'Are you she?' They recognize

13. "Spaßhaftes, Egmontgeschichten, Familienscenen mit Vätern, eine Hochzeit, kurz äußerst Liebenswürdiges" (Schumann and Schumann 1984–2001, 1:90).
14. "Das Concert, die Sonate, die Davidbündlertänze, die Kreisleriana und die Novelletten hat sie beinah allein veranlaßt" (Schumann 1904, 170).

each other" (Schumann 1946, 125).[15] A composition—say a piece for piano—that matches this paraphrase could have the following features. First, the structure, harmony, and melody must be very simple because of the social state of the two reapers. This we can see for example in the operas of Mozart, where the country girl Zerlina is given much simpler music than the court lady Donna Anna in *Don Giovanni*. In our fictive piece, the two reapers perhaps dance to typical waltz harmonies of tonic and dominant. Second, the question of the man might be composed as a contrasting middle section in the dominant (interrogatio). And finally, the recognition and identification may sound like a reprise or a motivic development, which leads to a specific goal. All in all, it might be a little waltz in three sections.

In reality, Schumann's paraphrase refers to the seventh *Deutscher Tanz* of Franz Schubert's op. 33 (D 783), which is a part of a masked ball (figure 6):

Figure 6. Franz Schubert, *Deutscher Tanz,* op. 33, no. 7

Now we can verify our suppositions through an analysis of the score. The first part (bars 1–8) is indeed very simple: the folk-like harmony, with the change of dominant and tonic every two

15. "Schnitter und Schnitterin, selig miteinander walzend. Er leise: 'Bist du es?' Sie erkennen sich" (Schumann 1836, 70).

bars, the periodic form, and the duet-like parallel thirds in the upper voices project an undisturbed, "happy" (selig) pleasure in the dance. In bars 9–11 we hear a dissonance (A♭/B♭), extended over two bars; this dominant-seventh chord expresses the desire of the two masked dancers to recognise each other, and the questioner's uncertainty sounds through the syncopated and limping rhythm in the left hand and the jarring modulation to the subdominant instead of the dominant. The soft question ("Are you she?") takes place in bar 12, as if direct speech that is conveyed with a changed musical language: a *piano*, legato, C minor, chorale-like texture with contrary motion in the outer voices. This singular contrasting bar is, however, motivically integrated through an inversion of the stepwise movement (c–d–e♭) from the second bar; this recollection of a previous supposition of the questioner prepares us for the identification. Finally, bars 13–16 represent the recognition by means of a motivic and tonal reprise; after the disruption in the middle section, the restitution of the waltz rhythm sounds like an identification of the music with itself.

Of course, we can also analyse and discover all the technical details of the composition without the poetic paraphrase. But I am not sure if we would find all these details in such a simple music structure without the subtle hints provided by the paraphrase. The self-evident, easily overlooked details carry a poetic meaning to which our modern ears must be sensitised. With his poetic paraphrase, Schumann lifted Schubert's "German dances" out of the low sphere of dance and *Gebrauchsmusik* to the higher genre of character pieces.[16]

All in all, an inverted analytical method which moves from the hermeneutic interpretation back to the musical structure has a great advantage: it promotes *musical* imagination and thinking in tones, and a composition is understood to be just one realisation of possibilities and not a solidified artwork. By seeking out the analytical implications of poetic paraphrases, the musical imagination can reproduce diverse compositional processes. Self-composed or

16. For the whole poetic paraphrase and its analysis, see Moßburger 2010.

imagined hypothetical scenarios create a foil against which the individual background and the particular solutions of the original composition can be recognised and appreciated.

CONCLUSION

Let us close with a final poetic paraphrase:

> At the same time, the whole thing is nothing but a serenade beneath the moonlight of the flageoletto sound, with notes carried over on the wind, from whence the beautiful trumpets blow and the trombone[, instrument of the last judgement,] answers with the promise of death. Then the martial drum calls for taps, disturbing the idyll, and the lover takes off with the mandolin still chirping away under his arm, while the beloved winks back at him with a violin figure.[17]

This very Romantic description of a wonderful moonlit night scene is inspired by the fourth piece from Anton Webern's *Fünf Stücke für Orchester*, op. 10, no. 4. You might be surprised, then, to learn that this Romantic poetic paraphrase is from none other than the structural hardliner Helmut Lachenmann (2003, 35). Despite the anti-Romantic campaign slogan "down with moonlight," poetic paraphrases could be made of any modern music that retains a lingering remnant of nineteenth-century traditions. And Lachenmann's spirited attempt, his little Romantic adventure with Gustav Mahler's vocabulary, may encourage us to continue the tradition of poetic paraphrases, whether by exploiting their analytical implications or by creating them ourselves, at least through the middle way of an analysis with musico-linguistic images.

---

17. "Dabei ist das Ganze nichts anderes als eine Serenade im Mondschein des Flageolett-Klangs, mit herübergewehten Tönen von dort, wo die schönen Trompeten blasen und die todkündende Posaune, Instrument des Jüngsten Gerichts, antwortet, bis die Militärtrommel zum Zapfenstreich ruft, die Idylle aufstört und sich der Liebhaber, die Mandoline unterm Arm weiterzirpend, davon macht, während die Angebetete ihm mit einer Geigenfigur nachwinkt" (Lachenmann 2004, 123). The bracketed insert is my addition to the 2003 translation to accommodate an insertion that Lachenmann made in the 2004 (second) edition of his Schriften.

REFERENCES

Bach, Carl Philipp Emanuel. (1753–62) 1925. *Versuch über die wahre Art, das Klavier zu Spielen*. Critical revised edition by Walter Niemann. Leipzig: C. F. Kahnt. Translated as Bach 1949. First published as *Versuch über die wahre Art das Clavier zu spielen* (part 1, Berlin: C. F. Henning, 1753; part 2, Berlin: G. L. Winter, 1762).

———. 1949. *Essay on the True Art of Playing Keyboard Instruments*. Translated by William J. Mitchell. New York: Norton. For further bibliographic details see Bach (1753–62) 1925.

Hoffmann, E. T. A. (1810–14) 1993. *Kreisleriana*. Edited by Hanne Castein. Stuttgart: Reclam. *Kreisleriana* first published 1810–14 as a series of individual text in various periodicals, principally *Allgemeine musikalische Zeitung*; republished in Hoffmann's *Fantasiestücke in Callot's Manier* (Bamberg: Kunz, 1814–15). Castein's edition first published 1983 (Stuttgart: Reclam).

———. 1814. "Alte und neue Kirchenmusik." *Allgemeine musikalische Zeitung* 16 (35–37): cols. 577–84, 593–603, 611–619.

———. 1989. *E. T. A. Hoffmann's Musical Writings:* Kreisleriana, The Poet and the Composers, *Music Criticism*. Edited by David Charlton; translated by Martyn Clark. Cambridge: Cambridge University Press. For further bibliographic details on *Kreisleriana* see Hoffmann (1810–14) 1993.

Lachenmann, Helmut. 2003. "Hearing [Hören] is Defenseless—without Listening [Hören]." Translated by Derrick Calandrella. *Circuit: musiques contemporaines* 13 (2), 27–50. First published 1985 as "Hören ist wehrlos—ohne Hören" (*MusikTexte* 10: 7–16), reprinted in *Musik als existentielle Erfahrung: Schriften 1966–1995*, edited and with a foreword by Josef Häusler (Weisbaden: Breitkopf & Härtel, 1996); revised as Lachenmann 2004.

———. 2004. "Hören ist wehrlos—ohne Hören." In *Musik als existentielle Erfahrung: Schriften 1966–1995*, edited and with a foreword by Josef Häusler, 116–35. 2nd ed. Weisbaden: Breitkopf & Härtel. 1st ed. published 1996. For further bibliographic information see Lachenmann 2003.

Moßburger, Hubert. 2010. "Die poetische Paraphrase als Wegweiser der Analyse: Zum Umgang mit musiksprachlichen Bildern am Beispiel Schuberts 'Deutschen Tänzen' D 783 in der Besprechung

Robert Schumanns." In *Musik und ihre Theorien: Clemens Kühn zum 65. Geburtstag*, edited by Felix Diergarten, Ludwig Holtmeier, John Leigh, and Edith Metzner, 161–71. Dresden: Sandstein.

Novalis. (1798) 1978. *Werke, Tagebücher und Briefe*. Vol. 2, *Das philosophisch-theoretische werk*. Edited by Hans-Joachim Mähl and Richard Samuel. Munich: Hanser.

Paul, Jean. 1804. *Vorschule der Aesthetik*. Hamburg: Friedrich Perthes. Translated by Margaret Hale as Paul 1973.

———. 1973. *Horn of Oberon: Jean Paul Richter's* School for Aesthetics. Introduction and translation by Margaret Hale. Detroit: Wayne State University Press. First published as Paul 1804.

Perrey, Beate Julia. 2003. *Schumann's* Dichterliebe *and Early Romantic Poetics: Fragmentation of Desire*. Cambridge: Cambridge University Press.

Rossbach, Sabine. 2008. "Mirroring, Abymization, Potentiation (Involution)." In *Romantic Prose Fiction*, edited by Gerald Gillespie, Manfred Engel, and Bernard Dieterle, 476–495. Amsterdam: John Benjamins.

Schoenberg, Arnold. 1978. *Theory of Harmony*. Translated by Roy E. Carter. Berkeley, CA: University of California Press. First published in German as *Harmonielehre* in 1911 (Vienna: Universal-edition).

Schumann, Clara, and Robert Schumann. 1984–87. *The Complete Correspondence of Clara and Robert Schumann. Critical Edition*. Edited by Eva Weissweiler. Translated by Hildegard Fritsch and Ronald L. Crawford. 2 vols. New York: Peter Lang. First published as Schumann and Schumann 1984–2001.

———. 1984–2001. *Clara und Robert Schumann Briefwechsel. Kritische Gesamtausgabe*. Edited by Eva Weissweiler and Susanna Ludwig. 3 vols. Frankfurt am Main: Stroemfeld/Roter Stern. Vols. 1–2 translated as Schumann and Schumann, 1984–87.

Schumann, Robert. 1835a. "Ferd. Hiller, XXIV Etudes." *Neue Zeitschrift für Musik* 2 (11): [41]–43. Reprinted in Schumann 1914, 1:43–46.

———. 1835b. "Hector Berlioz, Episode de la vie d'un Artiste." *Neue Zeitschrift für Musik* 3 (13): [49]–51. Reprinted in Schumann 1914, 1:82–85.

———. 1836. "Tanz." *Neue Zeitschrift für Musik* 4 (16): 69–71. Reprinted in Schumann 1914, 1:201–3.

———. 1885. *Jugendbriefe*. Compiled by Clara Schumann. Leipzig: Breitkopf und Härtel.

———. 1904. *Robert Schumanns Briefe. Neue Folge*. Edited by F. Gustav Jansen. 2nd ed. Leipzig: Breitkopf und Härtel. 1st ed. published 1886 (Leipzig: Breitkopf und Härtel).

———. 1907. *The Letters of Robert Schumann*. Edited by Karl Storck. Translated by Hannah Bryant. London: John Murray. First published 1906 as *Schumanns Briefe in Auswahl* (Stuttgart: Greiner und Pfeiffer).

———. 1914. *Gesammelte Schriften über Musik und Musiker*. Edited by Martin Kreisig. 5th ed. 2 vols. Leipzig: Breitkopf und Härtel. 1st ed. published 1854 (Leipzig: Wigand).

———. 1946. *On Music and Musicians*. Edited by Karl Wolff. Translated by Paul Rosenfeld. New York: Pantheon. First published 1854 as *Gesammelte Schriften über Musik und Musiker* (Leipzig: Wigand).

———. 1971. *Tagebücher*. Vol. 1, *1827–1838*. Edited by Georg Eismann. Leipzig: Deutscher Verlag für Musik.

———. 1998. *Robert Schumanns Mottosammlung: Übertragung, Kommentar, Einführung*. Edited with commentary by Leander Hotaki. Freiburg im Breisgau: Rombach.

Tadday, Ulrich. 1999. *Das Schöne Unendliche: Ästhetik, Kritik, Geschichte der romantischen*. Stuttgart: J. B. Metzler.

Wagner, Richard. 1873. "Zum Vortrag der neunten Symphonie Beethoven's." In *Gesammelte Schriften und Dichtung*, vol. 9, 275–304. Leipzig: E. W. Fritzsch.

PERSONALIA

WILLIAM BROOKS

William Brooks is Professor of Music at the University of York (UK) and emeritus Professor at the University of Illinois (US). He is a senior research fellow at the Orpheus Institute, where he also serves as editorial coordinator for the Orpheus series of publications. A composer as well as a scholar, his work in both domains concerns the setting, analysis, and declamation of texts, the history of American music (vernacular as well as cultivated), and experimental music and aesthetics. Recent publications include a pair of articles for the John Cage centenary in *Contemporary Music Review* and an extended series of compositions in response to W. B. Yeats's theories of declamation. He is currently working on a musical theatre duo for piano and violin and a book on Charles Ives.

EDOARDO TORBIANELLI

Edoardo Torbianelli received a diploma in piano and harpsichord in Trieste and then continued his studies at the Koninklijk Vlaams Muziekconservatotium in Antwerp, Belgium and at the Barabants Conservatorium of Tillburg, Holland. Among his tutors were Jean Fassina, Jos van Immerseel and Jacques de Tiège. His career as a performer includes appearances at prestigious European festivals and several recordings for Harmonia Mundi, Pan Classics, Phaedra, Gramola, and Amadeus, two of which were awarded a Diapason d'Or. The Gramola release Liszt and the Violin, with Austrian violinist Thomas Albertus Irnberger, received a diploma of honour from the Hungarian Liszt Society at the Gran Prix du Disque 2012. From 1993 to 1998 he taught at the Koninklijk Vlaams Conservatorium Antwerpen and since then has taught historical piano, chamber music and performance practice of the romantic and classical periods at the Schola Cantorum Basiliensis, Basel, and the Hoschule der Künste, Berne. Beginning in autumn 2014 he will direct fortepiano practice in the new Master's program at the Sorbonne University in Paris.

JEANNE ROUDET

Jeanne Roudet lectures at the Université Paris-Sorbonne, where she is responsible for the Masters course in the research and practice of early music for the fortepiano and is also a member of the Institute of Musicology Research (UMR 8223 IReMus). Her publications focus on musical aesthetics of the eighteenth and nineteenth centuries and the relationship between historical sources and the interpretation of the score. She is co-author with Jean-Pierre Bartoli of the book *L'Essor du romantisme: la fantaisie pour clavier de Carl Philipp Emanuel Bach à Franz Liszt* (Paris, Vrin, 2013).

HUBERT MOßBURGER

Hubert Moßburger studied church music, music education, music theory, and musicology in Regensburg, Detmold and Halle (Saale). He was awarded his PhD in 2000 from the Martin-Luther Universität Halle-Wittenberg for his study *Poetic Harmony in the Music of Robert Schumann*. From 2002 to 2004 he was an editorial board member of the *Gesellschaft für Musiktheorie*, and from 2003 to 2005 he edited the review *Zeitschrift der Gesellschaft für Musiktheorie*. After several lectureships, in 2003 he was appointed to a professorship at the Hochschule für Künste Bremen, and in 2012 he took up a similar post at the Staatliche Hochschule für Musik und Darstellende Kunst Stuttgart. His published essays about music and music theory cover topics ranging from the fifteenth to the twentieth century.

JEAN-PIERRE BARTOLI

Jean-Pierre Bartoli is Professor at Paris-Sorbonne University. His research and publications focus on musical exoticism, musical evolution and musical theory in the eighteenth and nineteenth centuries, and musical semiotics. He was one of the founders of the journals *Analyse musicale* and *Musurgia* and of the Société Française d'Analyse Musicale. He authored *L'Harmonie classique et romantique* (Paris, Minerve, 2000) and he co-edited the *Dictionnaire Berlioz* (Paris,

Fayard, 2003). A recent publication, co-authored with Jeanne Roudet, is *L'Essor du romantisme: la fantaisie pour clavier de Carl Philipp Emanuel Bach à Franz Liszt* (Paris, Vrin, 2013).

DOUGLASS SEATON

Douglass Seaton is Warren D. Allen Professor of Music at The Florida State University, where he has served as Coordinator of Music History and Musicology, and as Acting Assistant Dean for Academic Affairs and Director of Graduate Studies. His principal research interests are in the music of Felix Mendelssohn, the Classic/Romantic period, musical narratology, and relationships of literature and music. His dissertation dealt with Mendelssohn's compositional processes. He is the author of *Ideas and Styles in the Western Musical Tradition* (3rd edition, Oxford University Press, 2010) and *The Art Song: A Research and Information Guide*, and he is editor of *The Mendelssohn Companion*. He has prepared the scholarly editions of Mendelssohn's *Lobgesang* (Symphony No. 2), published by Carus-Verlag, and *Elijah*, published by Bärenreiter. His articles have appeared in the *Journal of the American Musicological Society, The Musical Quarterly, The Music Review, College Music Symposium, Ars lyrica, Choral Journal*, and *The New Grove Dictionary of Music and Musicians*, as well as in numerous volumes of collected essays. Professor Seaton is former President of The College Music Society and has served on the Council of the American Musicological Society.

EDITOR
William Brooks

SERIES EDITOR
Peter Dejans

COPY-EDITORS
Edward Crooks
Mark Hutchinson

AUTHORS
Edoardo Torbianelli
Jeanne Roudet
Jean-Pierre Bartoli
Douglass Seaton
Hubert Moßburger

LAY-OUT
Jurgen Leemans
designed by Filiep Tacq

ISBN 978 90 5876 9987
D/2014/1869/65
NUR 663